Ripples *from*
*the*Zambezi

Ripples *from* *the*Zambezi

Passion,
Entrepreneurship,
and the Rebirth
of Local Economies

Ernesto Sirolli

NEW SOCIETY PUBLISHERS

Cataloguing in Publication Data:

A catalogue record for this publication is available from the National Library of Canada and the Library of Congress.

Cover design by Miriam MacPhail. Photograph of the hippo by permission of Natfoto/ANT Photo Library, Australia.

Printed in Canada on acid-free, partially recycled (20 percent post-consumer) paper using soy-based inks by Transcontinental/Best Book Manufacturers.

New Society Publishers acknowledges the support of the Canadian government's Book Publishing Industry Development Program and the British Columbia Arts Council in the publication of this book

Paperback ISBN: 0-86571-397-9

Inquiries regarding requests to reprint all or part of *Ripples from the Zambezi* should be addressed to New Society Publishers at the address below.

To order directly from the publishers, please add $4.50 shipping to the price of the first copy, and $1.00 for each additional copy (plus GST in Canada). Send check or money order to:

New Society Publishers
P.O. Box 189, Gabriola Island, B.C. V0R 1X0 Canada

New Society Publishers aims to publish books for fundamental social change through nonviolent action. We focus especially on sustainable living, progressive leadership, and educational and parenting resources. Our full list of books can be browsed on the worldwide web at: www.newsociety.com

NEW SOCIETY PUBLISHERS   www.newsociety.com

COMMUNITY WORKS!

Ripples From The Zambezi is the first in a new series of books that highlight original and exciting contributions to the theory and practice of community economic development. At a time when the forces of globalization are impoverishing communities worldwide, COMMUNITY WORKS! aims to provide fresh perspectives on how to empower local and regional communities everywhere to increase self-reliance and build secure and prosperous futures for themselves.

COMMUNITY WORKS! is a collaborative initiative of three partners: Simon Fraser's Community Economic Development Centre, Vancouver City Savings Credit Union (VanCity), and New Society Publishers — all of whom are devoted to increasing the sustainability of communities.

The Community Economic Development Centre at Simon Fraser University helps communities initiate and generate their own solutions to their common economic problems, build long-term community capacity, and foster the integration of economic, social and environmental objectives. Its academic programs are available both in the classroom and by distance education. The Centre also operates a web site of permanent CED resources at <http://www.sfu.ca/cedc/>.

VanCity is a democratically run credit union, applying its financial skills and resources to serve the needs of its members while investing in the social, economic, and environmental well-being of the communities in which it does business.

New Society Publishers is an activist book publisher, its mission being to publish books that contribute in fundamental ways to building an ecologically sustainable and just society, and to do so with the least possible impact on the environment, in a manner that models that vision.

Feedback on the COMMUNITY WORKS! series is welcome, as are suggestions for further titles in the series. Please contact Christopher Plant at New Society Publishers by mail, or by e-mail at: chris@newsociety.com

DEDICATION

To
Fosca, Sara, Francesco, Gioconda and Ulinder

CONTENTS

ACKNOWLEDGMENTS xiii

FOREWORD by Mark Roseland xv

PREFACE by Peter Newman xxi

INTRODUCTION 1

Part One – The Past 5

1. Out of Africa 7
    The taking of Chirundu 7
    Is this development? 10
    Swords into snowplows? 10

2. The Technological Fix 12

3. Homo Cupiens — The Desiring Man 16
    What is development, then? 18

4. Out of the Mountain Cave Back to School 21

5. The Art of Shoemaking 24
    Just do it 24
    Find the passion 26
    Put it together 26
    The Fremantle Shoemakers' Cooperative 27

6. The Esperance Experience 29
    Never take no for an answer 33
    Can you do it again? 39
    It will never work! 42

7. The Esperance Model Applied 45
    Spreading our wings 47
    Can it work in America? 49
    Lincoln County 49
    South Dakota 53
    The frozen welder 54
    Victor 57
    To stay or not to stay? 59
    The coldest winter in 100 years! 59

The Badlands and other projects 59
Hastings, Minnesota 61
The urban challenge 62
Too much, too little 64
City logistics 66
Canada 66
Camrose, Stettler, and New Westminster 67
The big Australian 69

PART TWO – THE PRESENT 75

8. On Facilitation 77
Set the sail 77
On passion 78
On skill 80
Tourists and lovers 81

9. Training Facilitators 83
The victim 85
Action at last 87
Finally at work 88
The first project 90
The management trinity 92
Find the people, form the team 93
The helper helped 95
Network 96
The "back of the envelope" business plan 98
The true business plan 99
From pie in the sky to — real cake 101

10. A Word of Caution 103
Tê 105

PART THREE – THE FUTURE 107

11. Facilitation and Economic Development 109
The wealth of nations 110
What will not work 112
The map is not the territory 113
Providing infrastructures for development 116

12. A Quiet Revolution **119**

Facilitating education 122

What education? 123

Puberty 125

The master — the teacher 128

13. The Politics of Personal Growth **132**

The bureaucrat as a facilitator........................ 134

14. Epilogue — Civic Society, Social Capital, and the Creation of Wealth **139**

Civic economy 142

Civic humanism... 144

NOTES... 146

ABOUT THE AUTHOR 153

ACKNOWLEDGMENTS

This second edition of *Ripples* owes much to the readers of the first edition. They not only bought the book, they talked about it, they photocopied and faxed it around the world, they adopted it as a university text and at times engaged in a month-long hunt to locate the few elusive copies remaining!

The first edition was available courtesy of the Institute for Science and Technology Policy at Murdoch University in Western Australia. To Professor Peter Newman and the long-suffering staff of ISTP, my thanks for the care they took in publishing and distributing that first edition. To Peter, in particular, goes my gratitude for his encouragement and friendship.

Since moving to the U.S.A. in 1995, I have become indebted to a group of Canadians and Americans who have made it possible for eighteen Enterprise Facilitation projects to be initiated. To the board members of the Sirolli Institute — International Enterprise Facilitation™, La Donna Boyd, Yvonne Fizer, Scott Moen, Michael Lazar, Peter Newman, and Matha Sirolli, my thanks for volunteering their help. Their knowledge, support, and dedication has made working in North America much easier. To Yvonne Fizer, also on the board, my admiration for her passionate resolve to introduce Enterprise Facilitation to Canada. As Executive Director of the Sirolli Institute Canada, Yvonne is on a mission .... And I am forever thankful for it.

To John McLaughlin, of Hennepin County, Minnesota, who saw this vision in the city and gave our model a chance.

Bob Williams, of VanCity Credit Union in British Columbia, has been a constant source of inspiration. Bob is a social entrepreneur, always exploring new ways for civic society to emerge and prosper, and his commitment resonates and nourishes mine.

To my wife Martha, who is not at all surprised to be typing these revisions, go my thanks and apologies for changing homes/city/country three times in four years and for forcing her to learn to speak Minnesotan! She knows well that I couldn't be doing what I am doing without her love.

I have made every effort not to use sexist language. If you should find too many "he's", please forgive me — I assure you that I have tried!

FOREWORD
by Mark Roseland

In *Ripples From the Zambezi,* Ernesto Sirolli credits E.F. Schumacher for letting out a secret back in 1973: most development experts are clueless about development! Practitioners in the field should instead look at the real needs of local people and offer "intermediate" technological solutions in tune with local resources, means and culture.

Schumacher used the term "intermediate technology" to signify "technology of production by the masses, making use of the best of modern knowledge and experience, conducive to decentralization, compatible with the laws of ecology, gentle in its use of scarce resources, and designed to serve the human person instead of making him [*sic*] the servant of machines."

The intermediate or appropriate technology movement of the 1970s and 1980s addressed both "hard" and "soft" technologies. The "hard" technologies included such things as passive solar design; active solar collectors for heating and cooling; small windmills to provide electricity; roof-top gardens and hydroponic greenhouses; permaculture; and worker-managed craft industries. The "soft" or "social" technologies included revolving loan funds, community development corporations, co-operative business structures, and other aspects of what we now call community economic development. Sirolli's notion of Enterprise Facilitation fits into this tradition.

Sirolli argues that economic development has more to do with people than with so-called comparative advantage, more to do with our collective qualities as citizens than with the trees on our lands or the fish in our seas, more to do with the resources in our heads than those under the ground. Sure, wealth can be generated in the short-term by exploiting natural resources, but long-term prosperity can only be created by collective intelligence — working together, exchanging ideas, sharing technology and resources, and helping each other to do well. Our greatest assets are our energy, imagination, skill, and our commitment to good work.

Schumacher's last book was titled *Good Work.* Sirolli's ideas are rooted in this vibrant tradition, and they constitute good work.

#

It gives me great pleasure to welcome you to the first volume in the *COMMUNITY WORKS!* series. The *COMMUNITY WORKS!* series is a partnership between New Society Publishers, the Community Economic Development Centre at Simon Fraser University, and VanCity Credit Union. Who are these partners, what do they have in common, and why are they interested in publishing books on community economic development? A little history serves to illustrate our common ground.

The Community Economic Development Centre at Simon Fraser University in Vancouver, Canada also traces its lineage back to E.F. Schumacher and his seminal book *Small is Beautiful: Economics as if People Mattered.* After reading Schumacher, says Sirolli, "one could not escape one's own conscience any more ... we had better reconsider what we were doing in the name of Western Civilization." The Community Economic Development Centre emerged in the same spirit.

The Centre was established in 1989 to further the understanding and the practice of community economic development (CED). The Centre was founded based on an assessment of CED as it then existed in British Columbia, the needs of the province, and the strengths of the university. The assessment report was written by Schumacher's close friend and colleague George McRobie, author of *Small is Possible* (1981) and Chair of the New Economics Foundation in the UK, and David Ross, a highly regarded Canadian CED practitioner and co-author of *From the Roots Up: Economic Development as if Community Mattered* (1986). Their report noted:

> A twenty-year history of interdisciplinary programming, has lead to the creation of academic disciplines ... all of which straddle traditional departmental boundaries .... The formation of such a [CED] centre would be consistent with SFU's tradition of innovation, and of outreach to communities around British Columbia... It would provide a much-needed support system for CED within British Columbia at a time when such support is becoming a critical requirement. And because attention is now increasingly focusing on self-reliant local economies based on appropriate technologies, on both sides of the Atlantic and in the Third World, the activities of a centre concentrating on CED could hardly fail to have both national and international dimensions.

The Centre grew out of the active support of over fifty faculty members across many departments, as well as many community groups outside the university. The Centre's goal is to provide research, training and advisory services to the CED sector in British Columbia through a team of associates drawn from the university and CED practice. The Centre helps communities initiate and generate their own solutions to their common economic problems, build long-term community capacity, and foster the integration of economic, social and environmental objectives.

The Centre has active academic, research and outreach programs. Its objectives are to provide academic programs in CED, both in the classroom and through distance education; to stimulate the study of CED and the process of CED; to collect and provide information about CED; to carry out projects on CED in partnership with communities and agencies; to facilitate effective use of the University's resources in responding to requests for assistance on CED problems; to create opportunities for professional development experiences and programs for CED practitioners; and to establish working relations with similar centres internationally, particularly in developing countries.

#

During the Depression of the 1930s a few priests on the faculty of St. Francis Xavier University in Antigonish, Nova Scotia, led by Moses Coady, were organizing co-operatives through their extension department as "adult education." To address the grim plight of the area's fishermen and farmers, they established credit unions throughout the Maritimes. Organized on a community basis, in the context of a broad co-operative strategy, this grassroots co-operative organizing became known in Canada as the "Antigonish Movement."

This decade of economic depression in the rest of Canada became a shining moment for Nova Scotia. People from all over the world came to learn from Coady and his followers. When the Antigonish Movement reached its peak just before World War II, 19,600 people were studying self-help in 2,265 study groups.

The roots of Vancouver City Savings Credit Union (VanCity) are firmly anchored in the Canadian cooperative movement. VanCity was founded in October 1946, at a time when all existing credit unions were based on employment, ethnic, or religious bonds and therefore excluded many people from joining. Realizing the need for a broadly-based community credit union open to all, twelve forward-thinking individuals pooled their resources and created VanCity. Today VanCity has over 260,000 members and almost six billion dollars in assets. The credit union is highly regarded for its initiatives in areas such as corporate social responsibility, community and regional economic development, and support for charitable and nonprofit organizations. Included among its many innovative products and services are peer group and self reliance loans, which provide micro-entrepreneurs with capital to grow and expand their businesses; Community Investment Deposit loans, which support affordable housing and environmental projects; and a grant program which uses revenues from VanCity's family of creit cards to fund grants for community environmental initiatives.

#

New Society Publishers originally came out of the Movement for a New Society, an organization inspired by the work of Mahatma Gandhi, Martin Luther King, E.F. Schumacher, and others attempting to articulate a new direction for economic development that was not dependent on violence and exploitation, unlike the prevailing military-industrial economy. New Society Publishers began in Philadelphia in the early 1980s in response to the Vietnam war and the nuclear arms race. Its early titles focused on peacemaking, nonviolence, and feminism, later broadening to cover alternative economics, progressive leadership, and educational and parenting titles concerned with raising peaceful children. A Canadian office opened in 1990, broadening the range of work to include environmental, bioregional, and ecological design titles. In 1996, the company changed hands and locations, moving to Gabriola Island, British Columbia. It now focuses strongly on issues of sustainability and social justice, and its new areas of publishing include, for example, new forestry, conscientious commerce, and community-based economic development.

#

With this heritage and shared values, it is not surprising that the partner organizations in this series have sought to work together. The CED Centre, for example, already uses many New Society titles in its academic program, and New Society is the publisher of my books *Toward*

Sustainable Communities (1998) and *Eco-City Dimensions* (1997). VanCity and the CED Centre have worked together on several projects, including research, student internships, co-sponsored lectures, and so on. Joining forces to bring important new CED books to public attention is another exciting way for us to work together.

Ripples from the Zambezi was originally published by the Institute for Science and Technology Policy (ISTP) at Murdoch University in Western Australia. ISTP's Director is Peter Newman, one of Australia's national treasures in the field of sustainable development and a leading figure in the global effort to reduce automobile dependency. Upon learning I had joined the CED Centre, Peter promptly sent a copy of the first edition of *Ripples* from Australia.

At the time, and for a year or two after, I did not encounter anyone else who had heard of Ernesto Sirolli's ideas. Then one day I noticed that dozens of people in my CED circles were suddenly talking about about them. Someone had been to one of Ernesto's workshops, someone else had found and read the book, someone else was trying to bring Ernesto back for another workshop, people at VanCity were talking about the book, people from the Provincial Government were talking about it .... But, mostly, people who had heard about the book but couldn't find it were talking about what other people who also hadn't read it said they'd heard about it — for *Ripples* was not available in North America!

That problem is now solved. With the COMMUNITY WORKS! partnership, *Ripples from the Zambezi* can now reach the wider audience it deserves.

Mark Roseland, Director
Community Economic Development Centre
Simon Fraser University
Vancouver, Canada

April 1999

PREFACE

ERNESTO was nervous. I'd never seen him nervous before or since, but his passionate unbelief in bureaucracy was phasing him out. We caught the lift to the wrong floor and were curtly told to look at the indicators next time. NEW ENTERPRISE SCHEME, 14th floor — silly!

We were met with a practiced smile and shown to a seat, behind the safety of a large desk. Ernesto had stopped talking for some time now and looked very glum as I prattled on about his ideas for setting up new enterprises based on a person-centered approach.

An encouraging smile: "And what kind of products do you see being made by your new business, Mr. Sirolli?" Ernesto was now holding his head in his hands. A long pause, a sigh, eyes heavenward .... "Wooden automobiles ..." was the barely audible reply. "How very interesting."

Somehow the interview never got anywhere after that, so I picked up the forms to be filled out in triplicate and we fled to the lift.

Outside in the open air Ernesto laughed for nearly 20 minutes remembering the look on my face when he had dropped in the "wooden automobiles" idea. He then told me the story of the famous Morgan car which is still hand-built with a wooden frame in Malvern Link, England, and has a waiting list of ten years. To Ernesto it represented the ultimate in economic madness but human commonsense. "It's OK," he said. "The unemployment scheme is not for us. There has to be a better way — how about introducing me to your new minister/boss you keep saying is so good." "OK, we're having a few drinks after work; come up, you may be able to see Julian then" I replied.

This is a different scenario. It's a bit noisy, no desks, and Ernesto has an audience. The sparkle is there; he's performing: "If someone wants to surf all day, let him .... One day he'll want to do something, and then I'll help him. Passion is the starting point, skills can then be learnt, doors can be unlocked, and dreams can become reality."

"See what the department thinks," says Julian. So I set up a meeting with the economists who are a bit flummoxed but soon have it sorted out Ernesto explains:

"The problem is that governments can only influence employment through providing infrastructures and the right investment climate. Anything else is just manipulating the marketplace and is only artificial and bound to collapse when the government support is removed ..." and "job creation schemes are good public relations while unemployment is so high, but it's only when a large burst of capital is brought to an area that anything like a regional development center occurs ...."

The minister looked at me and paused for even longer than normal. "I don't think we know much about regional development; if we did, why is Perth so big and booming and most country towns so small and declining?" he said. He paused again. "I'd like to give Ernesto a try. He seems to have a spark. I like him. It's a risk but I would like to put him in Esperance to see if what he proposes works. If he can't make it in six months, we'll call it off."

I had a few reservations too. Ever since Ernesto had walked into my office at Murdoch I knew here was someone special. His ideas were not just good, they inflamed you; but did they work? He had to be given a chance.

The rest is history.

Nothing visible happened in Esperance for the first four months; the department asked the minister (unsuccessfully) to cut off funds. After six months the first light could be seen. After three years it was a national success story! "Can Ernesto come and do it here, please?" came from everywhere: Geraldton, Victoria, New Zealand, America. Of course by now the department had incorporated Ernesto's work as one of their established programs. But Ernesto could see that the essence of what happened in the development process was being lost.

From then on I urged him: "You have to write it down, Ernesto; if you're worried about how people will take the words and kill the substance, then you've got to set it out in your own passionate words. Go away somewhere. Go to America and write your book."

The world has many problems. This book contains some of the solutions.

PETER NEWMAN

Associate Professor in City Policy;
Director, Institute for Science and Technology Policy
Murdoch University, Western Australia

INTRODUCTION

For the past eighteen years I have traveled throughout Australia, New Zealand, the U.S.A., and Canada repeating a very simple message: "Right now, in your community, at this very moment, there is someone who is dreaming about doing something to improve his/her lot. If we could learn how to help that person to transform the dream into meaningful work, we would be halfway to changing the economic fortunes of the entire community."

It sounds far-fetched, doesn't it? A dream itself?

In 1985, I helped a previously unemployed person to set up a fish smoking plant in Esperance, a remote rural community in Western Australia with a population of 10,000 people. Some of the fishermen supplying him with tuna also had a dream and asked me to help them export their catch to Japan. When they succeeded, the farmers came with their dreams ....

An independent report prepared by the Commonwealth Office of Local Government had this to say about what was achieved in Esperance:

> "In summary, the achievements [of the Esperance Local Enterprise
> Initiatives Committee between 1985 and 1988] consist of contributions
> to the formation of 45 operating businesses, with a combined annual
> turnover of about AUS $7.1 million and directly adding 77 net full-time
> equivalent jobs to the economy."[1]

Since this report another 380 businesses have been set up in Esperance with help from the original Enterprise Facilitator, and many other communities have asked to be assisted in setting up a "Local Enterprise Facilitation" program.

Today there are some 200 communities in Australia, New Zealand, the U.S.A., and Canada that have a full-time "Enterprise Facilitator" available to them. This growth has been directly and indirectly inspired by what happened in Esperance.

Starting with Esperance, the growth of Enterprise Facilitation has resulted from word of mouth advertising and the testimonials of clients, community leaders, and facilitators involved in projects of great variety and range. From isolated rural communities in Western Australia and Central South Dakota to inner-city communities in Minneapolis and British Columbia, our belief in indigenous growth has been confirmed and continues to astonish those who witness it.

Compared to the early attempts to introduce Enterprise Facilitation to communities in 1985, the present work is considerably easier. It seems that entrepreneurship is going through a revival and that there is, at least at the grass roots, a renewed interest in self-employment. Maybe it is because communication technology allows people to work very effectively from their homes or because increasingly people experience the thrill of working in their pajamas!

There is also evidence of an emerging new class of entrepreneurs: women. Women set up 60% of all new small businesses in North America where in the last seven years they have created more jobs than all of the Fortune 500 companies put together.

Big government is on the way out, and big corporations retrench workers in both bad and good times!

What management consultants endearingly call "right-sizing" has left a generation of 40- to 60-year-olds out in the cold. Such people are so traumatized by the perceived corporate betrayal that they swear never again to put their livelihood in the hands of an employer. They may go back to work for a corporation but preferably as private consultants, making sure to have a diversified portfolio of clients.

Enterprise Facilitators can tell many stories of the quality and diversity of their clients. Among them are the young, the women, the retrenched middle-aged, early retirees, and angry ex-primary producers. They are in the market right now looking not anymore for just employment but also for a way to make a living without compromising their need for dignity.

Due to the changed economic environment, civic leaders are accepting more readily the notion of indigenous growth. With the exception of the few who still believe in massive infrastructure development and business attraction, there is a change in attitude and a questioning of the sustainability of buying "development" with public funds. "Corporate welfare" is under scrutiny, especially since globalization has made it obvious that corporations chase lower production costs regardless of the civic consequences.

The debate on economic sustainability has also benefited Enterprise Facilitation: The human scale of small enterprises, their bond with the community, the fact that they use proportionally more labor and intelligence than raw materials, makes them easy to propose to even the most environmentally conscious communities. One thousand home-based businesses cannot even be seen; a factory employing 1,000 people will change the physical landscape, even the air a community breathes. Emerging trends in customer demand also encourage smaller production units.

Customers demand variety, quality, service and ethics in business. Price is but one of the factors determining consumption. These new trends have spurred new ways of winning market share through niche marketing: personalized, customized, labor-intensive, intelligence-intensive, client-centered, highly localized, cooperative endeavors are but some of the techniques that small firms and individuals use to take on the corporate giants.

The last fifteen years have confirmed that governments and corporations do not create jobs. Jobs are created by small individual enterprises. It seems that today intelligence creates jobs and capital creates products.

Enterprise Facilitation is without any doubt the social technology of choice for job creation for the new millennium. Long gone is the nonsense about the "leisure society," dead and buried the dream of cradle-to-grave security of employment; what is here, stronger than ever, is human resourcefulness, passion, intelligence, and creativity. So much so that "passion," once the preserve of saints and artists, has started to be noticed, even encouraged, by management and their consultants. The latter, in their search for corporate excellence, are discovering, probably in total disbelief, that it is people, not formulas, who create and run successful firms, constantly reshaping the economic landscape.

Enterprise Facilitation was founded on passion and on the assumption that self-motivation, energy and, intelligence exist, right now, everywhere. They are like air, light, and oxygen. They are what allows the human species to survive and what ultimately will lead to the survival of our planet. To go from the smokestacks to the green stacks, to be able to feed, clothe, and transport five billion people in a sustainable way, we need another industrial revolution. We need millions of entrepreneurs producing differently and inventing the sustainable technologies, including the social technologies to do so.

We need therefore more, not fewer, enterprises. Who is creating the eco-industries of tomorrow? Enterprise Facilitation is working with thousands of individuals who are the salt of the earth, the people whose choices, acts, and decisions will shape the economic and social landscape of the communities they live in and possibly the world beyond.

People interested in my work ask two questions: "How does person-centered economic development work?" and "Where did I get the idea from?"

This book will hopefully answer both these questions by describing the genesis of the idea and by detailing the practical aspects which make its implementation both possible and successful. It also attempts to look at the future of facilitation and touches on the opportunities that a respectful person-centered approach can offer in the fields of education, health, and the delivery of public services generally.

The book is divided into three distinct parts: the past, the present, and the future.

"The Past" is part autobiographical, part anecdotal. It describes the genesis of the idea of Person-Centered Development and Enterprise Facilitation and its applications in Australia (Fremantle, Esperance, and Geraldton), New Zealand (Manaia and Taranaki), the U.S.A. (Minnesota, South Dakota, and Metropolitan Minneapolis) and Canada (Alberta and British Columbia).

"The Present" presents a how-to manual for the training of Enterprise Facilitators and is recommended reading for practitioners of Local Economic Development and Community Revitalization.

"The Future" explores the possibilities that the concept of Person-Centered Development can bring to fields such as counseling and education and examines its linkage with social economy and civic society.

PART ONE

THE PAST

1. OUT OF AFRICA

Ex Africa semper aliquid novi.

"There is always something new out of Africa."
— Pliny the Elder

THOSE WHO HAVE WORKED IN AN AFRICAN COUNTRY WILL TELL YOU, if they are honest, that they always learn from the experience much more than they had bargained for .... I am no exception, and I have to start this account by taking you back to the time when my personal "penny dropped" and I became aware that not all was well on the African development front.

I worked at the time (early 1970s) for ASIP, an Italian Agency of Technical Cooperation with African countries, similar to many other aid-abroad agencies the world over. We trained and sent volunteers to staff projects negotiated by the foreign offices of the relevant countries.

The taking of Chirundu

It was during a routine visit to one of our agency's outposts that I had the conversation which was to become so important to my thinking.

I was talking to one of the five volunteers who had been sent to establish a training farm near Chirundu, a Zambian hamlet on the Zambezi River, and he told me that for the first couple of months on the job they had had a real problem.

Their development plan called for thirty of the local men to work every day to clear the land in preparation for planting. These same men would, one day, literally "inherit the earth." They would be given possession of individual plots on the farm with use of the communal facilities, which included tractors, trucks, storage shed, seed, and other equipment.

It all seemed pretty straightforward but ... the thirty men, who worked so happily the first Monday of their future life, never came back! At least not for the next six days.

What became painfully obvious to the Italian volunteers was that the one Kwacha (equivalent at the time to one American dollar) they had paid the village men at the end of their first day of work was enough to buy 25 kilos of Milly Mill, the corn flour which was the staple diet of the village. Since they had plenty of fish from the river and game from the bush, the villagers simply didn't need to work more than one day per week.

How idyllic you would say! Well ... not quite.

The news was devastating for the Italian team. "What about outcomes?" they thought. "How are we to fulfill our obligations to the Italian and the Zambian governments, if the village's only work on Mondays?" They could imagine the five-year plan becoming a forty-five-year plan, with workers forever weeding the same field Monday after Monday!

"Let's cut their pay to twenty cents a day" was one immediate proposal. But this they couldn't do because the agreement with the Zambian government called for a minimum daily wage of one Kwacha.

What to do?

Then the five experienced Italian men, barely out of their teens, came up with, what they thought, was an original solution to that unusual problem. They got the local men to desire more money by encouraging them to buy what they, having recently arrived there from Italy, had in their possession. These consumer items included sunglasses, watches, transistor radios, beer, and yes, whisky.

In six months, I was told, Chirundu was conquered.

Now the men would work every day, with the exception of some who would not turn up on Mondays. The reason? You've guessed it: hangover!

I could not believe we were doing this. Here we were, talking about aid, technical cooperation, and caring for these people, and what did we do? We got them hooked on beer so that they would want more money and would come to work every day to get it.

I was too young then, though, to protest. Too naive to disbelieve their argument that what counted was results, not good intentions. I said nothing, convinced that in the name of achieving the five-year plan I would have done the same. I would have found the way to "motivate" the local people, I would have "made a success" of it, and I would have "fulfilled our objectives" no matter what .... But then I was taken to look at the tomato field and my Machiavellian beliefs received a mighty blow.

The fact was that there were no tomatoes to be seen anywhere. None had been harvested either, and yet the crop had by all accounts been spectacular. The selected tomato seeds brought all the way from Italy had responded to that virgin patch of African soil by producing gigantic plants, which promised a harvest to write home about. The lush and intensely green tomato plants had made a startling sight against the red soil and the blue waters of the mighty Zambezi—the river which flowed steadily only meters away from the new crop.

One fateful morning, at harvest time, the Italian volunteers had gone to the field to find nothing but great big water puddles where the crop had been. Nothing had been spared, and the field looked as if it had been dug up, at random, with a backhoe. Approaching the field the Italians, had disturbed the culprits of such devastation, and it didn't take long to figure out what had happened.

They could see ripples in the Zambezi!

The best-fed hippos of the entire river system were enjoying their after-dinner siesta literally a stone's throw away from what had been the pride and joy of the Italian contingent.

When I was told the story of the hippos, I laughed but then something really hit me. "What the hell are we doing here?" I said to myself. "Is it for these 'results' that we have hooked the community on beer and whisky?"

It might have been the beauty of the place, the smiles of the locals, I don't know, maybe some residual morality or even some intellectual propriety I, but from that moment on I started to look at our work in Africa in a different light. I became conscious of the fact that we were not doing the right thing — and consciousness is an extraordinary thing.

Is this development?

We may go through life without noticing what should be obvious to us, and then one day something happens and for the first time we see. Not only do we see it that day; we will see it forever. It will haunt us. It will not leave us alone.

My work with the Italian agency went on for a few more years but, my innocence haveing been lost, I could not stop myself from noticing how little we were doing to help the African people. Not only that, the more I looked the more I saw a jumble of disasters.

It wasn't only we Italians blundering our way around Africa, Asia, and Latin America. It seemed to me that most international aid projects were characterized by a pernicious kind of inappropriate development, which created more problems than it solved.

I will never forget an Algerian official who, disgusted by so-called Western experts descending upon his country, suggested that the Italian government should pay for the privilege of sending "experts" to learn something in Algeria.

Swords into snowplows?

Every Western country would take to Africa what they had, expecting to graft these "gifts" onto the African psyche.

The Italians bequeathed to Somalia their ridiculous bureaucracy which meant that a traveler who spent only a day in that country had to file, on exit, a taxation return in triplicate, typed in Somali on government-stamped legal paper.

The French sent teams of professors to the Ivory Coast to test local teenagers for the high school certificate. The test had been designed in Paris yet they wondered at the poor results of the locals.

The Americans did everything Big. They sourced out and donated thousands upon thousands of solar ovens to African tribes. The fact that the majority of them only cooked at night came as a bit of a shock!

The Russians also gave what they had. I cannot say that I actually saw them, but I was told by a number of eyewitnesses that for years it was possible to see two snowplows rusting at the Kampala airport!

But these were little things; what was going on behind the scenes was much more sinister. The history of international aid was also a history of corruption, debt, and moral bankruptcy.

Then in 1973 "Fritz" Schumacher published *Small is Beautiful,* and one could not escape one's own conscience any more. The secret was out: we experts didn't have a clue about what development was nor about how to foster it. From then on, we had better reconsider what we were doing in the name of Western Civilization.

And I did.

Schumacher's ideas were revolutionary. Fundamentally, he said two things to me:

1 If people don't ask for help, leave them alone.

2 There is no good or bad technology to carry out a task—only an appropriate or an inappropriate one. Something big, modern, and expensive is not necessarily best; it all depends on the circumstances.

2. THE TECHNOLOGICAL FIX

THE 1950s AND 1960s HAD SEEN THE TRIUMPH OF AN ARGUMENT opposite to that of Schumacher. Why wait for the Third World countries to slowly grind through their own industrial revolution, when we could give them modern technology? The concept of technological transfer was born.

Propelled by the magnificent results of the post-war Marshall Plan in Europe and Japan, the United Nations decided that what had been good for derelict Italy and a devastated Germany would be equally good for the Third World. Money was the solution, money to lend to the Third World so that technology could be bought.

What kind of technology? Theoretically good, solid, industrial technology: oil refineries, smelters, and transformation and manufacturing technology. In reality, with few exceptions, the technology sold by Europe and America to Africa and Asia was obsolete and, even allowing for a coat of paint, outrageously priced.

The International Monetary Fund, the World Bank, and the European Community Fund for Development all participated in creating the world's worst case of mass indebtedness, with an eagerness only matched by the various developmental agencies peddling their wares. African and Asian leaders were asked, prompted, and even told that they needed modern technology and then offered full services by the foreign agencies. The agencies did it all: from carrying out the feasibility study to preparing the submission to the funding agencies, to finally depositing money in a Swiss bank account on behalf of the president, monarch, or local minister.

The in-joke in Western financial institutions was that even before one piece of equipment reached its new destination, all the money was back in Western coffers and some of it was hiding in a Swiss bank account, paying interest to the Swiss for the privilege! **13**

Many technological projects, once implemented, became millstones around the necks of the purchasers. Broken parts could not be repaired locally and would need to be replaced with imported parts. Foreign technicians would be flown in from Sweden, Canada, Italy, France or wherever. Their rates were huge and expenses had to be paid in foreign currency. Their commitment to the country was minimal. The factory output would invariably be inferior to its Western counterpart. Indeed, some plants never opened.

The "laziness" of the locals was used to justify delays and incompetence. If and when production of the newly manufactured goods finally occurred, they were often too expensive for the local market, and being of inferior quality, unsuitable for export to industrialized countries.

If production was good and the company a success, even if it was subsidized, then it was beset with other problems. Factory workers, for example, would suddenly begin earning in a month what they and their had relatives previously earned in a year. A new class was created.

Money appeared in a traditionally moneyless society. The local culture often obliged the "fortunate" workers to care for their families; in many countries this meant sharing with "extended families." These families would move from the country to squat with the richer relative hoping, one day, to get a job in a modern factory. Thousands followed, abandoning the countryside. Did they lack food in their village? No, they lacked the money to buy the products that the new Western factories disgorged and advertised. The Lambretta, radios, and Coca Cola. These became the new status symbols that their corrupt or inept leaders had been conned and bribed into buying from Western development agency consultants.

In the meantime, as the national debt grew, cash crops would be quickly introduced to provide badly needed foreign currency for loans and further investment, thus institutionalizing a regime of never-ending dependency. For example, it has now been proven that the environmental disaster of the desertification of the Sahel had little to do with the "greenhouse effect" and much to do with the introduction of cash crops into that fragile ecosystem which had for centuries guaranteed the survival of the nomadic tribes.

14 A dual economy would develop: city and rural, at odds with each other. Not surprisingly, a series of reports commissioned by the United Nations at the close of the 1960s evidenced dismal results for the so-called "First Decade of Development." The poor became poorer, the rich richer, and the total foreign debt of Third World countries started to assume the proportions we have since grown accustomed to.[1]

In 1973, E.F. Schumacher's *Small is Beautiful* was published, a work which examined the developmental debate in an enlightened and truly original way. The subtitle *Economics as if People Mattered* reflected the author's real concern with people, not formulas. This concern, expressed throughout the book, obliged practitioners in the field of cooperation to look at the real needs of the local people and to offer "intermediate" technological solutions in tune with local resources, means, and culture.

Schumacher's genius was to dispel the myth that the tractor was the best technology to use. His point was that there is no perfect, absolute technology to produce a certain outcome. To till the soil, for instance, a hand-held wooden plow can be used; equally effective can be a steel plow drawn by horses, oxen, or camels and a four-wheel drive, air-conditioned tractor can also do the job. Schumacher argued that a technological change from a hand-held wooden plow to an animal-drawn steel one, for instance, assuming that the village blacksmith could manufacture and repair one, would bring greater improvement to village prosperity than the purchase of a tractor. A tractor may increase productivity but it would also bring debt and technological dependency.

The Western myth of the high-tech fix, of capital-intensive labor-saving devices, has proven to be counter-productive in many Third World regional economies. Imported technology forces the user into a debt trap wherein traditional methods of production are radically altered and the borrowers forced to produce more to repay the loans to buy the machinery to produce more, and so on.

Schumacher raised the alarm about the consequences of this vicious cycle. He also noted the trends of decline in Western economies and the attendant drift of population to the cities and degradation of the rural heartland.

But Schumacher didn't only talk about economics. By writing "If people do not want to better themselves, they are best left alone"[2], he challenged the view that helping others, whether as individuals or nations, is a moral **15** injunction and that by doing "good work" we are somehow bringing civilization to those who "don't have it." He thus questioned what we in the West assume to be our duty: to spread our industrial technology.

Small is Beautiful stressed that we should not take for granted our ability to identify other people's problems or to offer solutions which are appropriate to the situation. The message for me was to respect other cultures: we have to wait to be invited to share other people's problems, we have to listen with an open mind, and we have to leave behind our own prejudices and assumptions of superiority.

This wasn't an economist talking, or was it? If Schumacher was right (and I knew in my bones that he was), what kind of person would dare to get involved in economic development? I knew that many of the people I had met in so-called "developmental agencies" were very mediocre, even incompetent, and by Schumacher's criterion they should have been forcibly restrained from showing their faces in a Third World country.

Critics of the international aid agencies been many. The difference with Schumacher was that he seemed to talk about all of us, about people, as if we really mattered.

He closed his famous book with these words:

> Everywhere people ask: "What can I actually do?" The answer is as
> simple as it is disconcerting; we can each of us, put our inner house in
> order. The guidance we need for this work cannot be found in science or
> technology, the value of which utterly depends on the ends they serve;
> but it can still be found in the traditional wisdom of mankind.[3]

3. HOMO CUPIENS

THE DESIRING MAN

WHERE DO YOU GO WHEN YOU NEED TO PUT YOUR INNER HOUSE IN order? You find yourself a psychological mountain cave and you sit at the feet of a master. In my case, I took one year to read anything I could find which related, even marginally, to the problem of development.

When I came across Abraham Maslow's work, I realized that I had happened upon another thinker who not only could help me "put the inner house in order," but could also help answer all those other questions which my attempts to define development had generated.

Abraham Maslow's work as a clinical psychologist had taken a sharp and momentous turn when he began to reflect on the remarkable characteristics of some of the older and wiser individuals he had met. He wrote of these encounters:

> Such people seem to be fulfilling themselves and to be doing the best that they are capable of doing, reminding us of Nietzsche's exhortation, "become what thou art!" [1]

He became fascinated by the wisest, psychologically healthiest representatives of the human species and decided to study them. (A radical departure from traditional psychology and psychiatry, which seem to dwell on the disturbances or illnesses which bedevil humanity.)

His findings set him on a path of discovery which led to the formulation of a theory of a hierarchy of needs.

Maslow wrote:

> The study of such self-fulfilling people can teach us much about our
> mistakes, our short-comings, the proper directions in which to grow.[2]

Suddenly, "health" started to have a new meaning for me. Born into a
family of doctors, I had, until then, considered health to be a lack of
illness. Furthermore, a healthy person, to me, couldn't become "healthier";
that is, one could try and maintain health, but couldn't improve upon it.

Maslow set himself to prove that there are no limits to personal growth
and that it is intrinsically human to be "practically always desiring
something:"[3]

> Man is a wanting animal and rarely reaches a state of complete satisfac-
> tion except for a short time. As one desire is satisfied, another pops up to
> take its place .... Wants seem to arrange themselves in some sort of
> hierarchy or prepotency.[4]

As Maslow found, desires don't always surface from our unconscious in a
random way. First come the basic or physiological needs. These are the
strongest needs, the ones that relate to our physical survival: food, water,
and sleep. Needs so strong that when unsatisfied the entire present and
future perspective of the individual would change:

> For the man who is extremely and dangerously hungry, no other
> interests exist except food; he dreams food, he remembers food, he
> thinks about food, he emotes only about food. He perceives only food,
> and he wants only food.... For our chronically and extremely hungry
> man, Utopia can be defined simply as a place where there is plenty of
> food .... But what happens to man's desires when there is plenty of bread
> and when his belly is chronically filled? At once, other (and higher)
> needs emerge, and these, rather than physiological hungers, dominate
> the organism and when these in turn are satisfied, again new (and still
> higher) needs emerge and so on.[5]

The importance of Maslow's work for the theory of development is the
discovery that when the physiological needs are satisfied, the craving
changes from physical to psychological needs. In other words, once we
are not hungry, what concerns us most is not another quantity, such as
having something else other than food, but a quality: being something.

Once hunger is satisfied then safety becomes the pre-eminent non-physiological need. The need for safety then will take on the same intensity that the need for food has for the hungry.

Maslow further commented:

> If both the physiological and safety need are fairly well gratified, there will emerge the love and affection and belongingness needs, and the whole cycle already described will repeat itself with this new centre.[6]

Being loved is not the highest need, however having self-respect is. The fact that our partners or our parents love us is meaningless unless we are able to look at ourselves and feel satisfied with our own achievements; we need to be able to respect ourselves and be respected. Self-respect and the respect of others become of paramount importance for a secure and loved person.

And yet this might not be enough. We could have all of the above and still be unsatisfied. We might be healthy, loved, and respected, but if we are not doing what we know in our hearts we ought to be doing, then even being loved and respected is not enough. Maslow wrote: "A musician must make music, an artist must paint, a poet must write, if he is to be ultimately at peace with himself. This need we may call self-actualization."[7]

What is development, then?

If Maslow is right, then development is a never-ending process which has to do with the satisfaction not only of material needs but of the equally important psychological needs, which emerge as soon as the former have been reasonably taken care of.

It is no surprise then that Maslow would write that

> ... Economists, not only in the west but also in the east, are essentially materialistic. We must say harshly of the "science" of economics that it is generally the skilled, exact, technological application of a totally false theory of human needs and values. A theory that recognizes only the existence of lower needs or material needs. How could young people not be disappointed and disillusioned! What else could be the result of getting all the material and animal gratification and then not being happy as they were led to expect, not only by the theorists, but also by the conventional wisdom of parents and teachers, and the insistent gray lies of advisors."[8]

In this reference to economics, Maslow quoted none other than Ernest Schumacher[9] — were for me the circle was finally closed: I had been unable to define development because I was looking only at the fulfillment of basic material needs, and that didn't tell the full picture. Because of Maslow and Schumacher I came to understand that successful development has to do with the quality, not the quantities, of life.

At last I could make something of my experiences in Africa and understand that some of the indigenous people I had met had enough food not to be motivated by physical needs. They were secure and did love and had self-esteem in the same proportions Western people had, maybe even more. Some of them were beautiful, wise, self-actualizing people reaching for the apex of full humanness.

I could not stop thinking about what Gandhi had said about the world having the ability to satisfy everybody's needs, but not everybody's greed. It was true that some of the African people I had met consumed a fraction of the food that we Westerners eat and had no electricity, transport, or running water, but so what. They had enough food not to be motivated by need for it and were able to conduct a personally rewarding and socially active life. In a sense, the quantities of life are essential only up to a certain point; then they pale into insignificance and can even become a nuisance (Witness the two North Americans in three who are on a diet!).

Having accepted Maslow's concept that human needs and wants extend beyond the basic physiological requirements (food, shelter, etc.) and encompass the notion of self-actualization as well as Schumacher's compelling argument that technology is an asset to human growth and development only if it is appropriate to a specific situation, I was confronted with the question of what kind of structure, what kind of institutions would need to evolve to maximize the number of individuals growing to their full potential.

Walt Anderson, in a book entitled *Politics and the New Humanism*, wrote that

> "[a]lthough Maslow's political theory is not highly developed, his two main propositions come through clearly. These are (1) that, contrary to Freudian theory, the needs of people and the needs of civilization are not necessarily antagonistic and (2) that the possibilities of a society's developments are contingent upon the ability of its structures and its members to recognize and encourage higher human needs and the

potential for self-actualization. Therefore, social science, political dialogue, and public policy must recognize and deal with the needs other than the more basic material ones. These two propositions are workable guidelines, I believe, toward the development of humanistic politics and a humanistic political science.[10]

A humanistic political science? What a great challenge! If healthy individuals make healthy societies, shouldn't political scientists concern themselves with the structures that facilitate personal growth?

4. Out of the Mountain Cave Back to School

IN THE FINAL CHAPTER OF *TOWARDS A PSYCHOLOGY OF BEING*, Maslow wrote that

> [i]t can be assumed that classical economic theory based as it is on inadequate theory of human motivation, could also be revolutionized by accepting the biological reality of higher human needs, including the impulse to self-actualization and the love for the highest values. I am sure something similar is also true for political science, for sociology, and for all human and social sciences and professions.[1]

Do political scientists ever consider the possibility that society is nothing but a body of individuals with their needs, joys, sorrows, and wishes? In his article "The Cheerful Science of Dismal Politics," Christian Bay, a political scientist, put forward this opinion:

> "I am convinced that our profession will never help us to advance from our wasteful, cruel, pluralistic pseudo-politics in the direction of justice and humane politics until we replace political systems with concepts of human need and human development as the ultimate value framework for our political analysis."[2]

The acceptance of a concept which sees individuals potentially growing forever could, I realized, inspire a revolution of Copernican magnitude. The force inspiring our existence can be found in the depths of our souls, and the flowering of our potentiality could become the process where we come to terms with our existence and participate in its wonder.

Without a belief in the intrinsic goodness of human nature, however, and without a humanistic perspective, one would find it impossible to advocate a society that encourages the fulfillment of individual needs for growth. Inspired by this thought, I started to research the writers who put the needs of the individual first and worked from there outwardly. I discovered that beyond society, class, and ideologies, a host of philosophers, thinkers, poets from all cultures and all ages had addressed the issue of becoming "what we are" and of the responsibility that we have to honor our humanness and live our lives accordingly.[3]

These thinkers subscribed to a positive vision of human beings who can grow healthy and strong and fulfill their true nature if the "sun" of love and the "water" of respect is made available to them. They made it possible to envisage a sociology of health whereby people's personal talents, if fulfilled, not only would lead to people's growth, but also to them becoming healthy and therefore "good" citizens.

After a while a picture started to emerge which was different from anything I had entertained previously. I began to conceive a vision of a society that facilitates personal growth by assisting individuals in achieving what they wish to achieve. A Taoist bureaucracy which does nothing until asked, and a great deal afterwards. A "humble" public servant who doesn't plan how to build the ideal society but who is enchanted by the unique, idiosyncratic needs and abilities of the people that he serves and whose task would be to respond to individual requests for assistance and provide the elements needed for that person to flower.

Piece by piece an antidogmatic, anti-idealistic picture started to take shape in my mind.

Most influential to my thinking at the time was Carl Rogers, the founding father of person-centered therapy. During years of effective therapeutic work, Carl Rogers very clearly demonstrated that it was possible to help people "heal themselves" by simply "being there," listening, facilitating, and responding to the client's needs for communicating and finding values to live by.

An antidogmatic, anti-idealistic society would, by necessity, have to be antiauthoritarian. In other words, it would make no sense at all to proclaim the freedom and self-respect of our fellow human beings and then to assume control of their lives by dictating how they should live and behave. He described his method as one in which "the individual and not the problem is the focus."[4] The aim is not to solve one particular problem but to help the individual to grow so that he can cope with the present problem and with later problems in a better, more integrated fashion. Rogers' therapy was not a matter "of doing something to the individual" but rather "of removing obstacles so that he can again move forward."[5] This therapy relies on the intrinsic "wish to grow" of which Maslow spoke, and on that peculiar human characteristic which urges us to realize our potential and to fight for our fulfillment.

In Rogers' words, some of his unfortunate clients resembled pale potato sprouts germinated in a cellar where light only filtered from a window high up on the wall. The "wish to grow" was still there in those pathetic little sprouts, but the conditions were such that what germinated was only the specter of a healthy sprout. Similarly, in some of his clients Rogers could see the stunted potential, the pale image of the person which "could have been" if the "sun of love" and the "water of respect" had been available.

Rogers, Maslow, and the various adherents to psychological schools and currents of thought loosely named "third force psychologists" all believed in a common trait of human personality. They believed that the pathology, the sickness in human behavior, was the result of stunted growth and that the restoration of health had to do with the creation of an environment conducive to further growth.

Could Rogers' facilitator be adopted as the model for the bureaucrat of tomorrow's society? Could we use the facilitator to remove obstacles so that people could become adults and take care of their lives, children, jobs, towns, and countries? Did we really need to be governed by a paternalistic, dogmatic body like "those in authority?"

Two things happened to me at that time. The first was that I started to develop a great distaste for authoritarian and manipulative people; the second was that I felt like doing something practical to demonstrate that facilitation could be applied to other fields of endeavor. I wanted to engage myself in the world with renewed hope and faith, and I soon developed an idea of how to do it.

5. THE ART OF SHOEMAKING

READING ABOUT THE CHAMPIONS OF THE HUMAN RACE, I COULDN'T avoid creating, in my mind, a demonology — that is, a list of the demons oppressing us.

Contrary to Dante's "Inferno," however, my hell wasn't populated by naked gluttons, greedy merchants, and assorted petty sinners. The torturers had no tails; rather, they were well-dressed authoritarian figures who, in the name of an idea, would torture and beat the psychological life out of the people in their power. From unyielding bureaucrats to religious fanatics, from political extremists to rabid do-gooders, my demonology started to contain anybody who dreamt up a code of conduct and tried to manipulate or coerce others to follow it.

How could I demonstrate that people, if helped to become what they truly wished to be, would blossom into beautiful beings, create wonderful work, contribute to their families, communities, and society in a loving and caring way? How can one prove that such potential exists in the hearts and minds of all of us?

Just do it

I looked at my own community, the City of Fremantle in Western Australia, and decided that this was a good place to start. My aim was to demonstrate that simply by going with the energy and imagination of people, helping them to achieve whatever they wanted to achieve, we would be able to satisfy both their personal and the broader community needs.

Fremantle has a lively food and craft market. During the late seventies, an "alternative" community still traded their "flower power" wares. These wares included some sandals, which had the finesse and durability of something out of the darkest period of the lower Middle Ages. Naturally they did not sell well, and yet the happy cobblers would persist in offering them along with equally poorly crafted belts, wallets, key rings, and personalized beer can holders.

Among those trying to make a living out of leatherwork there must have been a few who truly loved their work and were frustrated by their lack of real craft skill. Did they make any money? I doubted it and I said to myself: "What would happen if people who loved working with leather were given a chance to learn to become very good leather workers?" What if their passion was matched by skill?

I was able to receive some funding (AUS $900) from the City of Fremantle, job-creation being a constant preoccupation of politicians the world over. I decided to start the project by finding someone in the community who could teach "hippies" how to make shoes that people would buy. A visit to several bootmaking shops led me to contact a surgical boot workshop attached to a major hospital. There, I was told, was the man I was looking for: the dean of local shoemakers, the unchallenged master, was — oh joy! — Italian. Then aged 66, Dino Pezzino had migrated to Australia in the early 1950s from Sicily. He had been in his trade then for over 50 years, having started his apprenticeship at 14 years of age in his uncle's workshop.

Our first meeting was a friendly one. As I described the effort that I had witnessed going into producing awful sandals that nobody wanted, I asked him if he had ever thought of teaching. His experience of the apprentices sent by state agencies convinced him they were unwilling to learn and uninterested in work, so he had given up the idea of teaching long ago.

I asked him if he was prepared to try again, but this time we would approach it the traditional Italian way: I would introduce trainees to him, but he would have the final say as to whether he wanted to teach them or not. He had a good laugh at that and agreed. He concluded our meeting by telling me how much he wanted to pass on his art. "You know," he said, "I should have retired last year, but the hospital couldn't find anyone to replace me; they have even advertised in England for orthopedic shoemakers; here there are no schools to teach shoemaking."

Find the passion

I had to find people with a passion for leatherwork. I started with the Fremantle markets and was introduced to a girl in her twenties. I went to visit her at home to ask if she was interested in learning shoemaking. She admitted that she had had enough of trying to make a living selling sandals. For years she had asked bootmakers to teach her, but no one had been willing to employ her as an apprentice. "My sandals are pretty bad," she said with a self-deprecating smile. "I feel awful when my friends buy them because I know that the stitches will fall apart in six months, and then so will the sandals." I explained that as a case study I was trying to demonstrate that people, if assisted in doing well what they love doing, not only make a living but, by becoming happier, also make society better.

I told her that I had found the best master shoemaker in town and that we were ready to set up an informal training session if that was what she wanted. She was very interested to meet Dino and gave me the name of another frustrated cobbler friend. In a week, I had assembled five people, all unemployed, their ages ranging from 20 to 45 years. My frustrated cobblers had been making cheap, low-tech goods, on and off, for over six years! — and all of them wished to do better.

Put it together

Longhaired, bearded, sandal-shod, earring in one ear, both ears, or through the nose, my newly found apprentices looked like anything but! Crammed into a car, we arrived at Dino's ornate villa looking like gypsies lost in suburbia. We were admitted to his garage, which doubled as his workshop.

There standing in front of his workbench, a prehistoric Singer sewing machine to his left and a pile of leather to his right, Dino grinned at the approaching throng and said, "So, you want to learn how to make shoes? Come, come, I will show you." In his hand he held a beautiful pair of green high-heeled shoes he was making for a lady who had one foot slightly shorter than the other. The heel was really high, the shape a classic "stiletto," pointed and elegant.

I will never forget the faces of my Australian friends. Here were people who had spent hours, days, months bent over a piece of leather, trying to make a blasted pair of sandals that even with the strongest glue would fall apart in weeks and there, smiling at their amazement, was this beautiful old man who could do what they never in their wildest dreams thought they may be able to do. I felt at that moment what the educational psychologists call the "aha experience" — the sudden understanding of how things work, the revelation which hits a person who couldn't understand and then ... aha ... can see, can realize.

As I watched, the would-be apprentices went into "workshop mode" as instinctively as ducklings take to water. The tools were touched, appreciated; the simple contraptions created over hundreds of years of experience were deeply understood. Good, simple, effective tools were lifted, touched, and caressed. "That's how you do it," one murmured, "I once wanted to make myself a pair of boots but because I didn't know how to use lasts, I stitched one while wearing it on my foot. It looked all right, but I couldn't take it off, so I had to cut it off!"

There was a lot of laughter and excitement at that first meeting. Dino seemed delighted at the eagerness of the new pupils and committed himself to teach them, for free, twice a week, for as long as it took. They in turn pledged $5 each per week to pay for Dino's transport.

I pledged to find a workspace and to assist in whatever way possible. That was how the Fremantle Shoemakers' Cooperative started. Most of my research money went into purchasing an old sewing machine and an even older finishing machine, five knives, five hammers, pliers, nails, etc. The Fremantle City Council gave us the use of a large basement room under a furniture factory in the older part of Fremantle. The council reglazed some windows, connected the power, and provided paint and brushes to whitewash the walls.

The training started in earnest a month after my meeting with the administrator of the council. I took him and the mayor to inspect the first city-sponsored "long-term job creation scheme" and they were speechless.

The Fremantle Shoemakers' Cooperative

Speechless with delight. So was I, and I would have been more so if I had known then that the $900 project would last ten years, train two dozen people in varying degrees of skill, and propel some of them into further careers in orthopedic shoemaking, special footwear, and even an academic degree in podiatry.

At the time I was simply satisfied to be there, to help with the cleaning, only to be allowed to witness unhindered learning and growth. I watched Dino teach how to sharpen a knife and then proceed to cut a sole out of a thick piece of hide nailed to a wooden last with one uninterrupted motion of his arm and wrist. I then watched as he nailed another piece of hide to the same last and invited an apprentice to copy him using his own knife. He couldn't do it. This particular apprentice had been working the longest with leather and even taught some leather work, but he had not known how to sharpen a shoemaker's knife. When he understood, he threw away in disgust the flimsy blade wrapped in plastic he had been using.

During the ensuing year more people wanted to attend the classes. Some stayed for years, some learnt how to make simple but beautiful sandals and left. The learning was free, the organization minimal and democratic in the fullest sense.

To me, the experience was the beginning of an impassioned search for ways to make "good work" possible and the confirmation of the theories of the "people believers."

6. THE ESPERANCE EXPERIENCE

IT IS NO USE TELLING PEOPLE, YOU HAVE TO SHOW THEM. AND YOU can only show something when you have done it. To do it, you have to take risks, inject yourself with the experimental vaccine and wait ....

After the experience with the shoemakers, I wanted to scream to the world "It works!" and I desperately wanted to do it again, to see the smiles of people who understood what was happening to them. The excitement, joy, and self-respect which results from putting committed people in touch with each other and with the skills that they so badly wanted had made a deep impression on me.

Family and work reasons took me away from Fremantle, however, and it was only on my return to Western Australia four years later that I was given the opportunity to try this on a larger scale. On the strength of my previous work and the publicity that a television documentary on the Fremantle shoemakers had given me, I was introduced to the Minister for Regional Development whose electorate included Esperance, a remote rural community 800 kilometers to the south of the state capital.

Esperance was suffering yet another of the seemingly perpetual rural economic downturns. The minister's advisors bundled me into a charter flight with the assignment of taking a look at the place and telling them what my thoughts were. I accepted the challenge gladly even though I knew that they did not understand what I wanted to do in Esperance. In fact, I suspected that if they had really understood, they would have never put me on that plane!

It took forever to arrive there!

Esperance is a very isolated rural community in Western Australia. It is perched precariously on the edge of the Nullarbor Desert, built on granite boulders, which are constantly hammered by the roaring Southern Ocean. Off its coast there are 160 islands, mostly inhabited by sea lions. Then south of those islands nothing until Antarctica. To the north miles of scrub sand dunes, then 450 kilometers away the twin cities of Kalgoorlie-Boulder. To the west again sand and salt, lakes of it, and a further 450 kilometers away another town of 20,000 people: Albany. To the east only desert for a thousand miles. No real neighbors to talk about.

In 1985 Esperance, was going through a difficult time. It was the height of a rural recession, and Esperance with its sandy, salty soil had one of the highest rural debts in Australia. The fishing industry was also in recession. After years of free-for-all, catch-as-much-as-you-can, the tuna population had started to decline and the federal government had introduced a quota system, which had played havoc with the local industry. The fishing fleet had gone from 45 to 7 boats, and those fishermen remaining were the ones with the lowest quota available and the highest debt. At the time, Esperance had a population of 8,500 people, with another 1,500 living on the surrounding farms. Five hundred people were registered as unemployed, with youth unemployment nearing the 20% mark.

I arrived in Esperance with a lot of faith, but not much else.

My faith was in people, and in their universal characteristics of wanting to become something, of enjoying good work, of achieving respect and self-respect, by performing beautifully. I had faith that in Esperance, like anywhere else in the world, there would be individuals that at that very moment were dreaming, discussing, even sketching on their kitchen table their ideas for that special something they wanted to do. I knew, not only with my head, but with my heart as well, that the only thing I had to do was to become available to those people and to "facilitate" the transformation of their dreams into good work.

But where would I find those people if I didn't know anybody there? I was left in town by the ministerial advisors who flew back to Perth on the same day after giving me a list of names of locals who might help me, a car to drive, and keys to the minister's empty house.

The following three days I spent meeting some of the local people who were either professionally or voluntarily involved with local development. My question to them was always the same: "Do you know anyone in town 31 who is currently thinking of becoming involved in setting up a business?" Their answer was always the same: "No!" Some would elaborate by saying that that was precisely the reason for Esperance's unemployment. The farmers and the fishermen were in strife and nobody would risk investing locally. Of the local unemployed people, some would say they were too lazy and too well looked after by the government to be willing to work.

Not convinced, I asked the manager of the local Youth Support Scheme to organize a meeting with the unemployed who used the center. At that meeting two young people came out. One had just arrived in town and the other one was about to leave; neither had any idea for self-employment.

The manager of the Commonwealth Employment Services organized a similar meeting. Out of 500 registered unemployed, two long-term unemployed people came to that meeting. One didn't know what to do, the other one had been struggling for months trying to set up a fish-smoking business. He had built a $250 smoking kiln in his garage and started selling some fish, but he had only succeeded in having his smoked fish confiscated and his embryonic business strangled by bureaucratic red tape.

He was angry and terribly frustrated but I couldn't stop smiling.

After five days and four long nights I had found my first client: somebody in Esperance who wanted to do something! Having been retrenched from a local fish-processing plant, Mauri Green, a skilled fish processor, formerly from "fish wise" New Zealand, had attempted to overcome his predicament by doing what came naturally to him: processing fish for sale. He had built a smoke oven in his garage, smoked fish, and started to sell it ... and collided head-on with the local health inspector. A former friend, the health inspector tasted the fish, liked it very much, but proceeded to confiscate it on the grounds that Mauri's garage did not comply with health regulations.

Not having any money to move his smoke oven to an approved building, Mauri had tried to gain the support of local and metropolitan industrial development bureaucrats. His request for assistance had failed to dent the elephantine skin of those supposedly in charge of small business development. His enterprise was considered insignificant compared to "real" economic development and Mauri had been given the treatment that all aging unemployed who tinker in their garages would get — a terse dismissal.

To me, Mauri was "the" first client, the person who had passion, skills and who needed somebody to help him to transform his dream into legitimate, rewarding, and fulfilling work. Mauri was like one of the Fremantle shoemakers who wanted to make shoes. The difference was that he had the skill already and that I didn't have to find a master to teach him. I simply needed to help him set up a workshop for him to go about his art. I was so excited at finding him that I had to forcibly repress my enthusiasm and make sure of his intentions.

After dozens of questions, I asked him if he really wanted to make a living by smoking fish. I emphasized the "really" and he looked at me puzzled, then he asked me why I wanted to know. I told him that if I put all my energy behind his idea, he could end up to his neck in smelly fish, and if he didn't love that life, I would rather not help him do something he might later regret. He looked at me in disbelief — fish was his life, his love, and he was passionate about it. That sealed our working relationship. Fish was for Mauri what leather was for Dino, and I could stop worrying and start working with this man.

My first week in Esperance was nearly over, and I had no written report (again) of what could or should happen; instead I had a person's dream in my hands to show those who had commissioned my research.

The Minister for Regional Development arrived back in Esperance for the weekend. Away from his office and telephone, he had time to talk to me. His wife and thirteen-year-old daughter joined the conversation. I told him of my belief in people and their ability to create wonderful products if they were only given the chance to do so. I described to him my unease with "top-down" solutions or "big" economic development plans, which tended to discard or overlook the small but exciting possibilities found locally. We talked about quality value-added production to complement the quantity export of primary products constituting the bulk of Australia's economy. I showed them the pair of kangaroo hide shoes I wore made by Dino. "Why are Australians exporting two million salted kangaroo hides every year when they could produce shoes of this outstanding quality here? How many Australians are aware of the fact that the most expensive

Italian shoes are of this extraordinary kangaroo leather? There are people right here," I told them, "people who have the passion to create products, goods, new markets, and quality services, and who, if believed and encouraged, could become a vibrant contribution to the economy, providing diversity of employment and renewed hope for the rural sector!"

33

We had by this time adjourned to the local Chinese restaurant where, after two hours of passionate discussion and fiery food, I was given a one-month contract to become available to anyone in Esperance "who wanted to do something"!

Never take no for an answer

My first project was to get Mauri's smoked fish business off the ground. He needed to get a loan, and I contacted on his behalf the government agency that had rejected his application.

The person at the other end of the telephone "only worked there" and, no, he couldn't tell me the reason for the first rejection. I was told that a committee made the decisions and that its proceedings were confidential.

My reply was that Mauri was a long-term unemployed person, that his activity and status fitted precisely the agency's guidelines, and that I wanted to resubmit personally the application to the next committee meeting. He told me that that was out of the question, and I replied that unless some cooperation was shown by his department, I could find out, through the Freedom of Information Act, the reason for the rejection and I would not hesitate to go to the press if I found any discrepancies between his department's guidelines and the committee's allocation of public funds to the long-term unemployed. At that point, his tone of voice became more conciliatory and he told me that, even though it was confidential, he would tell me the reason for the loan refusal.

The committee, he said, thought that Mauri's activity would compete with the local fishermen. I must have screamed into the phone because the guy at the other end went very quiet. "He is not competing with the fishermen, he is buying from them, and adding value to the fish and selling it again. Can you please explain to your city people's committee the difference between fishing, which is done with hook and line, and smoking, which is done with heat and flames!" The application was resubmitted and after a month a very nicely written letter and a check for $4,000 arrived.

A shed in the industrial area was rented and, after consultation with the health inspector, a minimum amount of partitioning and special fittings were installed. Mauri then took the home-built kiln out of his garage and, with the help of a couple of friends, set it up in the newly partitioned shed. His operation was legitimate and Esperance Fish Processors was born on the right side of the blanket!

An official opening was organized at which much beer-smoked fish and emotion were displayed. Naturally the Minister and Local Member was center stage and was obviously enjoying the first fruits of my work.

Nearly three months had gone by since my first visit to Esperance. While working with Mauri, I had asked a number of local people to help me by forming a support committee. I wanted local people to be fully informed of my activities and to assist me in finding local resources for my clients. I also wanted them to spread the word around about my availability to work, in total confidentiality, with any local person who wished to set up a new business or to expand an existing one.

In those first few months maybe a dozen people approached me. Among them were two tuna fishermen who, having witnessed my work with Mauri, decided to see what I could do to help them. And help they needed since the federal government, concerned about the decline in fish stock, had imposed a drastic cut in their quota. The tuna industry was in the doldrums.

Unfortunately, the two fishermen came independently of each other and I had to come to terms with the fact that the local fishing community was not only in economic trouble, but also distrustful and divided, with its members still hurting from a cooperative venture that had failed miserably only a year before. Good mates at the pub, the local tuna fishermen didn't want to work together any more and faced their industry's decline in bitter isolation. After speaking separately with those first two fishermen, realized that their problem was exacerbated by the low price their tuna was fetching. They only had one buyer, a tuna cannery, which had a monopolistic control of their industry and offered them sixty cents per kilogram for any quality tuna. There had never been a market for high quality tuna and the fishermen had traditionally been pushed to fill their boats with as much tuna as possible regardless of its size or condition. A truck from the cannery would await the boats at the pier, and the bloodied tuna would be simply thrown into steel boxes and taken away.

The drastic cut in the tuna quota had meant that instead of 60,000 tons, the Australian tuna fishermen were left with only 14,000 to fish. Of these, the Esperance fishermen only had the right to less than 140 tons, which left them with a combined annual gross revenue of less than $300,000, hardly enough to keep up with their boat repayments.

I expressed my concern to both fishermen I spoke to and suggested that a meeting be organized with the other five tuna fishermen to seek a common solution. They shook their heads at that idea and made it clear that, short of a miracle, nothing would make them work together. It took a good three months for the "miracle" to eventuate. I met more fishermen at Mauri's business launch and had the impression that my work there had not gone unnoticed. Finally, one morning five of the local fishermen came to see me. I had the immediate impression that they had begun to work together because they had a strategy already worked out and were ready to try it on me!

I was working for the government, they said, and I should go back to the government and tell the people in charge that they had destroyed the tuna industry. "Now," they said, "the only hope is to catch big tuna for the Japanese market." But money was needed for a big boat and research, and they wanted me to get it out of the government. The argument was delivered with great passion and, at one stage, fists were slammed on the table to make clear their contempt for the ruthless government int ervention. I told them that my task as a consultant was to help Esperance people and that I would have my contract renewed only if I succeeded in doing so. My loyalty, therefore, was with them and I wanted to help, but my understanding of their predicament was different from theirs and so was my proposed course of action. I knew that the government had already given a research grant to fishermen on the south coast to find the elusive big tuna to be air freighted to Japan. The results had been dismal, and I doubted that the government would give them a $150,000 grant to try again. I also told them that their reputation as fishermen was very poor and that the Fisheries Department bureaucrats considered them to be young, unruly "cowboys" among the tuna fishermen.

They looked totally deflated. If I wasn't a government representative and if I wasn't willing to make a representation on their behalf, then what was that meeting all about? I told them that unless they could find alternative markets for the small tuna they had easy access to, they would never be better off. Instead of trying to develop a fishery for the mythical big fish, they should carry out marketing research to dispose of their usual catch at better prices. They asked me how much it would cost to do a marketing study and I told them that the question wasn't how much a marketing study would cost, the question was how much they were prepared to invest in one. They looked at each other, thought for a while, and finally the figure of $200 each was agreed upon. If they had been ready to ask for a large amount of money from the government, when it came to their dollars, the amount had shrunk considerably. Nonetheless, with $1,000 pledged I advised the five to pen a common bank account under the name Esperance Sashimi Development Group, "sashimi" being the term they had used in our discussion on the highly priced tuna which the Japanese eat raw. Next I advised them to publicize and be proud of their newly found solidarity, and I told them that I would try to find some matching finance to assist with the marketing research.

This I did and, as in the case of Mauri, I didn't get any satisfaction from approaching any of the various government agencies and assorted development corporations, which are supposedly there to help small business. Nobody wanted to get involved with the fishermen, and I was told repeatedly that those fishermen were "cowboys" who only fished when they felt like it, were uncommitted, would not cooperate, and could not be trusted. Such comments were repeated by local people who made it even harder to seek support for the project.

Finally, all other avenues being exhausted, I turned to the Local Member and asked for a matching $1,000 from his ministerial discretionary funds. He was willing to encourage the fishermen to work together and promptly obliged with a check. This gesture had a profound effect on the fishermen and, indirectly, on the town. Somebody trusted them, and the previously unruly and unmanageable fishermen became, from that day on, a different bunch who would show Esperance people a thing or two.

While the money was being organized, I asked the director of the local technical college, who was a keen member of my support committee, whether he could finance a sashimi fish handling demonstration for the benefit of the fishermen, Mauri, and local restaurateurs. It would require finding a willing Japanese chef and paying for his fees, travel, and expenses to come to Esperance. In his inimitable style that excellent man had the funds made available and a ticket donated by an airline the same day.

I found the Japanese chef in Perth, and a couple of weeks later we had a big day at the Esperance Youth Hostel, or rather in its kitchen. About 20 locals came to see the visiting chef at work and admired his skills in preparing a tray of sashimi and a tray of sushi made exclusively with fresh fish provided by the Esperance Sashimi Development Group.

What happened that day would have effects far beyond our joint expectations and would change not only the fishermen's attitude but also Mauri's fish smoking practices and showed how we could create wealth from Australia's resources by value-added practices.

The fishermen had provided the chef with a 10 kilo tuna, which was average size for their catch. The fish was about one-sixth the size of the tuna that reached fabulous prices in Japan. At the end of the elaborate and meticulous preparations, we were invited by the chef to try the sashimi. One of the fishermen asked him if in fact that could be called sashimi because in the videos and other documentation he had seen only very big and very fatty fish were used in preparing that particular dish. He, and in fact all of us, were surprised to hear from our instructor that sashimi meant "raw" and that the term had nothing to do with size or type of fish. Many varieties could be used to prepare that traditional and highly sought-after dish. Fat tuna, he said, was considered by the Japanese to be the most exquisite food and big tuna fetched as much as $200 per kilo. But small tuna, if killed and handled to Japanese standards, were widely used in sashimi preparations.

All of a sudden it dawned on the fishermen present that what they had been selling to the cannery for 60 cents per kilo could be sold to the Japanese for sashimi. The question, which was on everybody's lips, was finally asked: "Do you mean to say that your restaurant would buy small tuna from us?" The answer was "yes, this is small but very fresh, very good tuna." "And how much do you think your restaurant would pay for it?" came the immediate second question. The answer was $3.50 per kilo, nearly six times the price paid by the cannery.

At that moment, there was a long combined whistle of all those present, and I could hear the noise of their brains calculating! If all their catch could be sold at that price, the value of their catch would shoot to nearly three million Australian dollars which would be more than they made before the introduction of the federal quota. In other words, they would be able to catch less and make much more.

In Mauri's case, witnessing the work of the Japanese chef gave him the idea to smoke tuna fillets and to try this new product versus the more conventional whole fish he had previously used. His experiment with the local tuna combined with his skill in using native local woods for flavor created an extraordinary product which launched his smokehouse into the gourmet market in the capital cities of Australia; it also created an additional market for the tuna once destined for the cannery.

Not long after that momentous sashimi demonstration day I had the task of finding a consultant willing to undertake the marketing research for the Esperance Sashimi Development Group. Knowing that the "experts" in the Department of Fisheries considered the project unfeasible and that $2,000 could not buy me much time of an established marketing firm, I remembered a person whom I had met months before, and called him.

David Leith had come to meet me on the advice of a mutual friend who knew of my work with Mauri. David was at that time a frustrated public servant who was longing to leave his job if only he could find something challenging to do. Of New Zealand background, he had memories of his grandfather smoking fish, and the story of Mauri, as told by our friend, had made him want to meet me even though he had nothing specific to ask me or to propose. At the end of our first meeting he told me that he would love to get involved with anything to do with fish and that, if the occasion presented itself, I should not to hesitate in calling him. On the chance that he could be willing to take up the daunting task of rescuing the Esperance tuna industry I called him and explained the situation. David became interested and, as he then worked full-time, offered to come to Esperance during his Christmas holiday. The amount of money available was really small, but that didn't concern him. What worried him was the fact that he had never seen a tuna in his life. But he would do his best for the fishermen if they were prepared to take him for what he was, somebody with an economics background but with no experience in marketing fish.

I told him that, as the experts had given the project no chance at all we knew that his mission was "impossible" and we would settle for the best that he could so. A meeting was organized, and I introduced David to the fishermen with these words: "This is David. He has never seen a whole tuna in his life, and he is here to help you!"

And help he did. Following up our experience with the Japanese chef, he introduced the project to all the Japanese restaurants in Perth, only five at that time, and then he rang all the other Japanese restaurants across Australia. Convinced that a market could be found, he took four months leave from work, borrowed $10,000 from his bank, and signed an exclusive contract with the fishermen. He took the product to Singapore where it sold for AUS $11.70 per kilo. He then resigned from his job, set up his own company, and, at the start of the new fishing season (eight months after his first meeting with the fishermen), sent five fish to Japan, where they were individually auctioned. After one week a telegram came back from the Japanese distributor saying "fish A1"!

The following week a representative from that company came to Esperance and, in partnership with another large tuna fishing company from South Australia, an agreement was reached for the establishment of a sashimi processing plant in Esperance. The new plant was built in twelve weeks and, that fishing season, 140 tons of tuna was air freighted to Japan at the average price of a cool $15 per kilo!

We all had big smiles on our faces that season. The impossible had been done and the skeptics, both in Perth and Esperance, had to eat their words. Mauri's smoked tuna and the Esperance Sashimi Development Group became the "good news" items not only in the local press but also in the state papers. As if by magic, Esperance was no longer a town in recession. Things were happening there, the name of Esperance being heard, and the locals, all of them, including those who had never believed that their own neighbors deserved to be trusted and helped, basked in the glory.

Can you do it again?

The success of the sashimi enterprise was a turning point in my work in Esperance. Before the opening of the sashimi plant, I had been approached by quite a number of individuals but never by the "establishment," that is, the wealthy local business people and farmers. The publicity that surrounded the launch of the new fishing venture, however, was such that some of the farmers started to take notice.

One of them expressed the feeling of the entire farming community by saying to me: "If those idiots of fishermen can do a thing like that, there must be something really wrong with us farmers." He was referring of course to the inability of farmers to take control of their products and to make more money adding value to them.

It was in recognition of what those "idiots of fishermen" had achieved that I was asked by a farmer to help solve the recurrent problem of getting rid of the old ewes, the mutton that nobody wanted and that was so difficult to dispose of.

Year after year millions of old ewes would hit the market during the same months and the price would collapse to the extent that often farmers who sent the ewes to market for sale at auction not only wouldn't receive a cent, they would be billed for the transport!

Mutton was another seemingly insoluble problem and, unlike the tuna, affected hundreds of farmers in the Esperance area and tens of thousands Australia-wide.

I asked the farmer who sought my help whether he wanted to research the problem individually or as a group and he told me that, since it would cost money, he would try to get some of his "mates" involved. He got back in touch with me with forty-eight other farmers who pledged $100 each towards a feasibility study to try to find a way of not losing money disposing of the old ewes.

My task was to find somebody to do the job, and this time I had no qualms whatsoever about approaching "nonexperts", having discovered, through David's experience, that experts often knew too much to be able to look at old problems with fresh eyes.

Ted Lefroy and John McComb had an interesting and varied background with degrees in agricultural economics but no specific insight into the marketing of mutton. In their early thirties, they were both self-employed and willing to try their hand at the job.

During the months that followed they came up with a specific business plan which transformed a certain yearly loss into net profit. Their plan had the remarkable title "NEW USES FOR OLD EWES," and it looked at commissioning the local abattoirs to slaughter the old ewes for a fixed fee and to return the bodies and skins to a farmer-controlled company. The meat would then be processed into small-goods and the skins, after being chemically depilated, would be pickled and sold. Finally, the wool would be sold as a separate and valuable item.

The most extraordinary part of the plan was the latter part. Traditionally the ewes would be sent to slaughter or to the markets after being shorn at the cost of $1 each. Ted and John's suggestion was that the ewes be slaughtered with their wool on. The wool would be removed chemically after the slaughterhouse had returned the skin. Sold at auction, the wool produced by this method would fetch eight percent less than shorn wool but, since it came from a dead animal, it was exempt from the payment of 10% duty on shorn wool. With this system, not only would the farmers save $1 by not shearing, they would make two percent more out of their old ewe's wool.

John and Ted demonstrated to the farmers in the group that the combined value of the small-goods, skins, and wool added up to a tidy profit and reminded the farmers that, if they wanted to work together, they could find solutions for even seemingly intractable problems.

More creative ideas began to flow from this innovation.

Twenty-seven farmers came together to look at what else they could possibly do to stop soil erosion and utilize their marginal land. They financed another remarkable study conducted by one of their former "enemies": Keith Bradby, the most vocal of the local environmentalists!

Keith was a very active local "greenie" — a radical environmentalist who had been influential in stopping new land releases in Western Australia. He had enormous love and respect for the local native flora and was able to show the farmers that the scrub, which thrived on their marginal land, had the potential to provide wildflowers and seeds, which had a commercial value.

Another project was then launched. Soil salinity and erosion plagued Esperance farmers to the point that ten percent of each farm's land was considered "marginal" — not fit for agriculture. With the assistance of Keith, local awareness of the delicate ecosystem grew so much that a special course in revegetation was organized by the local technical college and sixty-five people enrolled.

My greatest satisfaction came from a remark made by the president of a local farmer's organization who for years had been carrying on a written feud in the local paper with "greenie" Keith. "You know," he said to me, "for years I have been fighting with Keith, and I can hardly believe that tomorrow he will be coming to visit my farm, paid by me, to tell me what to do on my marginal land!" I had started to trust the locals, and now they had started to trust each other.

One year after my first day there, the news from Esperance was good and didn't go unnoticed. All the way from Canberra, a representative from the Federal Department of Local Government and Administrative Services, which dealt with regional development, came to visit Esperance. He offered to finance the employment of a full-time Esperance local enterprise facilitator to learn from me, to work for one year, and to keep documentation of this "pilot project" in rural economic development for the benefit of other communities.

The offer was accepted, but not without some misgivings from my committee which, jokingly, complained of the impossibility of finding "another Ernesto" and attributed my success to "being Italian, having a moustache, and moving my hands a lot!" I told them not to despair because if brain surgeons could be trained so could facilitators, and I was very keen to train the person they would decide to employ.

It will never work!

Brian Willoughby, not a drop of Italian blood in his veins, was their choice. Then in his early forties, Brian was born in a small town not far from Esperance and had settled in Esperance after working for many years as Town Clerk in numerous Western Australian rural towns. He had applied for the job thinking that he would be working as an economic development manager, a role that he felt fit to fill because of his planning and managerial background. He had been told that I would provide some training, and, considering that he was older and more experienced in Australian rural country towns than I was had submitted to it gracefully.

His first training took twenty minutes and was done in the car. "Brian," I told him, "there are only two things that I don't want you to do in this job. Anything else you can do but don't ever initiate anything and don't ever motivate anybody."

He looked at me as if I had just arrived from Mars, and then he explained to me that the reason why the committee had appointed him was because of his ideas about what should happen in Esperance and his determination to make it happen. I had to explain to him that what interested the federal agency was to see whether somebody other than me could implement a "responsive" approach to economic development and that his funding depended on us "piloting" this new approach and documenting its outcome.

He was unconvinced and complained that nobody would come to see him and that it would be a total disaster to rely on the locals for ideas. I asked him to write in his diary that on his first day of work he had told me that "nobody" would use his services. Disgruntled and annoyed, he told me that he would do what I had told him, that is, "nothing," until given different instructions.

43

True to his word, Brian never initiated anything or motivated anybody. He set up office in a tiny room on the main street of Esperance and furnished it with one desk, two chairs, and a cardboard box to be used as a filing cabinet. After two months, he asked for a week off. He had forty-six clients and he was going, in his words, "mad."

He could not believe that there were so many people who wanted to do so many different things. What surprised him didn't surprise me. I had been in that town for nearly one year providing a useful, free, and confidential service to the locals; it was to be expected that the Esperance people would keep using the service. Brian did recover from his initial shock and became not only an excellent facilitator but also one of the strongest advocates of the grassroots, responsive approach pioneered there.

With Brian "on board" and the committee more than happy with his results and attitude, we thought of organizing a public event to celebrate the achievements of the local enterprise committee. The event would publicize the fact that Esperance was fighting its way out of the recession, promote the local entrepreneurs and their products, and drum up enough support to convince the state government not only that Brian's position should be renewed but that his work should be promoted in other country areas.

Politicians, senior public servants, and press and business people came together for a day of celebration. The catering for that day was fantastic. Everything the guests saw and tasted was produced in Esperance. The "mutton group" had a Moroccan chef to cook hundreds of kebabs as a promotion for their product. Mauri's smoked tuna quickly disappeared from the tables, and so did a large quantity of fresh sashimi prepared by a local restaurateur who had learned from the Japanese chef how to prepare it.

Local wildflowers were beautifully displayed and so were twenty or so large framed pictures of local businesses recently established. Some of the businesses were really small but that didn't seem to matter. What mattered was the way the community had come together with courage and lots of spunk and pride—something rarely experienced in Western Australia in times of recession.

Our official guests were impressed. Not only was Brian's position to be refinanced by the state government, I was approached by a politician present that day to start a local enterprise development project in another rural country town nearly a thousand miles north of Esperance.

Brian, the members of the local support committee, and I were very excited at the idea of being able to repeat our experience in a different community. One of the criticisms was that our approach had worked in Esperance because Esperance's people had "special" entrepreneurial skill. We knew that that wasn't the case, and we were spoiling for the chance to prove it.

I couldn't conceive a better way of spreading the concept than repeating it and proving its worth.

Certainly there was a risk that some of the original spontaneity, excitement, and community ownership could be diminished by having a government department funding the project and taking more and more control, but what was the alternative? Until and unless the facilitator can be employed with funding coming from local government, the alternative is "big brother" funding with all the red tape that state and federal government funding imply. At that time, to repeat the experiment in Geraldton seemed too good a chance to miss — and this opportunity provided us with the experience to systematize what was learned in Esperance. As it happened, with another Brian ....

7. The Esperance Model Applied

REVIEWING MY EXPERIENCE IN ESPERANCE AND USING THE HELP OF Brian, I sketched a set of guidelines for the establishment of the local enterprise committee in Geraldton and for the employment of the facilitator. I never doubted that other rural communities would adopt the "Esperance Model" and was aware, at the time, of the political implication of the adoption of such a model in preference to the more traditional economic development strategies. I was excited, however, by the prospect that one day many communities would employ a facilitator who would help as many local people as possible to help themselves. In a sense, I was now called to do what I had dreamed of as a student, that is to come up with a set of rules to "institute" a mechanism whereby the highest possible number of individuals were assisted in doing what they wished to do. Some important questions needed answers: How could we institutionalize the facilitator's role without killing it? What were the elements that made this "servant of the public" not a "public servant"? Some of my friends, especially those who had experienced the frustrations of political activism in the sixties, were very concerned about my intention to institutionalize the role of the facilitator.

Another Brian got the job in Geraldton. Brian was a local businessman who, having successfully retired at the age of forty, had been sent back into the arena by the stock crash of 1987. When he saw the advertisement for the position, he felt that he had always been doing what was requested in the duty statement, and in all honesty, it took very little time to "train" him to be a facilitator. The idea that he was not to initiate things or motivate people was agreeable to him. He explained his attitude by saying that in his experience in small business he had learned that only those who were determined to succeed had a shot at it and those people didn't need any motivating. Brian Keeble thus became the second facilitator in Western Australia. He was responsible for assisting a community of 20,000 people, some 300 miles north of Perth, which included some of the oldest farming land in the state. Brian had no hesitation in embracing his new role, and I hoped that he would help us in demonstrating that what had happened in Esperance wasn't an accident and that person-centered economic development had well and truly arrived. I saw this work not as a theory but as a workable model capable of being adopted and success-fully implemented by diverse communities.

The reward for our work came under the guise of an independent study commissioned by the Federal Department of Local Government and Administrative Services that had financed the employment of the first Brian in Esperance. We suggested to the two academics who conducted the study on Esperance that they also look at the Geraldton project to compare the two. The results were very encouraging. Forty-five new businesses had been created with the assistance of the Esperance facilitator during the period 1985-1988. In Geraldton in nine months

> to the end of April 1988 there were 227 cases in which contact had been made with the Facilitator by people wishing for assistance from the [Geraldton Local Enterprise Facilitation] Committee with enterprises. Keeble split these cases into two categories: those concerned with completely new enterprises (172 cases); and those concerned with the takeover of existing enterprises or with general business advice only (55 cases). Combining these categories we may say that by the end of April there were 34 enterprises actually operating in the Geraldton Midwest region which had received some kind of help from the Committee or more precisely from Brian Keeble .... The 34 actual enterprises above represent a total direct net addition of 74.5 full-time-equivalent jobs in the economy. The combined annual turnover of these 34 enterprises (extrapolating from 9 months to 12 months) amounts to about $4.33 million.[1]

Obviously the people of Esperance were not exceptionally enterprising as the approach worked in Geraldton as well. In fact, it worked better there.

Spreading our wings

By December 1987, only 30 months since my arrival in Esperance, the Western Australian government had passed a proposal for the establishment of five pilot programs in "Local Economic Development Initiatives." The government submission stated in part: "With the growing interest by communities across the State, particularly in the model established in Esperance, it is desirable that Government support be established on a basis which is perceived as coherent and stable."[2]

In the following years the number of communities which received funding for the establishment of a local enterprise facilitation project in Western Australia grew steadily to 36. "Esperance" was also the model for the creation of two non-governmental agencies in that state: The Rural Innovation Center, whose aim is to assist primary producers wishing to diversify their operations; and the State Enterprise Center, whose primary aim is to "facilitate the development of individual businesses throughout Western Australia by providing support to the network of enterprise consultants."

In December 1988, the Victorian state government introduced the "Rural Enterprise Victoria Scheme" (REV). The scheme was "composed of two distinct but closely linked operations, one at the local level, the other central. At the rural community level the scheme consists of six full-time-equivalent enterprise facilitators operating in small rural towns/communities with the assistance and backing of community based committees .... To complement and support the local functions, the REV scheme includes a mechanism at the central level which will provide a focal information point for the facilitators."[3]

If Australian state government ministers were personally responsible for the rapid dissemination of the Esperance model, it wasn't to be repeated in New Zealand where the introduction of the model resulted from the vision and the initiative of a local government authority: the Waimate Plains District Council, formed by the merger of Waimate West County and the Manaia Town Council. This small authority of 215 square kilometers had a population of less than 3,000 situated in the southwest tip of New Zealand's northern island.

In 1987, when the District Manager traveled overseas to visit relatives, his trip was partly funded by the Waimate Council to investigate entrepreneurial activities in which local government or communities were involved. It was during his world tour (Australia, Sweden, Great Britain, U.S.A.) that I met Mr. Whitehead accompanied by his wife Genneth. We had a lengthy discussion, and I provided him with some written information on Esperance and introduced him to Brian Willoughby.

Upon his return home, he reported to Waimate Plains Council:

> Most of the community employment projects were top heavy. Local authorities were over involved and they were telling people what was good for them. Sirolli's approach was different—he was letting people do what they were interested in doing. Sirolli is coming from the other direction. He wants people to tell the authorities what they want to do with their lives and then they do it a damn sight better![4]

Mr. Whitehead was so convincing in his endorsement of the Esperance model that the Waimate Plains Council called a public meeting to assess local interest in the idea and subsequently approached Brian Willoughby for his assistance in recruiting and training the first New Zealand facilitator.

The enthusiasm, commitment, and determination of the Waimate Plains Committee was such that during the first of the three weeks spent by Brian in New Zealand funding was secured, a facilitator was appointed, and an office established. During the two weeks that followed, Brian and his first trainee, Neville Forman, had already been approached for assistance by 40 people.

The first report on the introduction of the program stated that "between the 23rd May (when Mr. Willoughby arrived) and the 25th July through the facilitator's office — 61 people sought assistance with business ideas — of these 7 new businesses were started and 33 were possibilities."

During the first three years of operation the Waimate Plains facilitator, covering an area with a population of 35,000 people, reported the following:

Total office contacts	736
Business start-ups	207
Estimated jobs created	400
Potential savings in unemployment benefits	$2,638,200[5]

In 1989, another facilitator joined Neville and "the pair helped initiate a further 12 business facilitator models in New Zealand from 1990-1991."[6] Figures from December 1998 estimate 70 communities in New Zealand employ a local enterprise facilitator/consultant.

49 ▶

Can it work in America?

Upon my first touchdown on American soil I had terrible misgivings, and I thought, "What can I possibly tell the Americans that they don't already know?" After all, American thinkers had inspired so much of my work. I felt intellectually inept and humbled at the sight of that great country. My invitation as Manager of the Western Australian Rural Innovation Center was an exchange visit to innovative farming projects in the Midwest: Minnesota, Iowa, Wisconsin, Michigan, and Indiana. My American sponsor was "Communicating For Agriculture" and they had selected an American rural development lecturer from Iowa to be my guest in Western Australia for a month.

On my final day in the States, I met Keigh Hubble, a board member of "Communicating For Agriculture"; lunch became an extended four-hour meeting! Keigh is a professor of Rural Education at Southwest State University, Minnesota, and a fervent advocate of a rural lifestyle and of rural values. His Norwegian background gives him strength and a delightful sense of humor, which he uses to propel his students to excellent work.

It was Keigh who urged me that day to return to America and to set up a pilot project in enterprise facilitation. He formally invited me to spend six months establishing a pilot program in Lincoln County and to start writing this book. One year after our first meeting I was back, with my wife and newborn baby, ready to tackle rural Minnesota.

Lincoln County

When I first told my new colleagues at Southwest State University that part of my job was to set up enterprise facilitation in Lincoln County, they laughed. "Poor bastard," they said, "certainly whoever thought of sending you there is pulling your leg, because nothing ever happens in Lincoln County." I was then told that Lincoln County "is not the end of the world," but that "you could see it from there!"

Situated on the border of South Dakota, one of the poorest rural states in America, it shares its problems — and problems it has. It is the poorest county in Minnesota and the longest-running in losing population (commencing in 1929, the exodus has reduced population from 20,000 to 6,800). It has the oldest population in the state (average age 42.5 years) and a per capita income of US $8,300 per annum. It has one of the highest farm debts, the lowest economic diversification, and, in the largest of its four towns (which go from a population of 180 to under 2,000), the latest census showed that 150 people were 85 years of age and older!

To top it all, I arrived at the beginning of WINTER — and nothing in Italy, Africa, or Australia can prepare you for winter in Minnesota!

Before I arrived I was told on the phone to expect zero degrees — naively I imagined snow, skiing, log fires .... I realized too late that Keigh meant zero degrees Fahrenheit, not Celsius. This means minus 20° Celsius an average of 0°. The temperature can go as low as minus 40° C (and it did a few times). My romantic ideas of snow-decorated log cabins by the lakes got a mighty blow when new-found friends gave us manuals on how to survive blizzards, car survival kits, advice about how to drive on black ice (don't!), and a table to add the windchill factor to the forecast temperature. (A windchill factor of 40 knots added to a temperature of minus 40° C will snap-freeze you for posterity.)

Lincoln County was frozen solid for most of my first time there. Literally the ground freezes and no earth-moving work occurs during winter. Being mostly flat prairie with little tree cover for protection, the country is well known for its potentially lethal "white outs," huge snow drifts and howling wind storms which can cover and freeze a car within an hour (some 57 people had died in this way four years earlier). When I was finally driven through Lincoln County, surprised me: it looked much worse than I had imagined! I had thought the Australian outback was barren ... but when I saw the Midwest prairie in winter, I changed my mind.

The four Lincoln County representatives who accompanied me were at great pains to explain why the county was so depressed and talked about the physical features passing us by—they didn't know I was not interested in the local geography.

Their suggestions for suitable economic initiatives included fencing the entire county and reintroducing the American buffalo for game meat and allied industries.

I let them talk during that first guided tour but whenever I was introduced to a local, I would inquire about their activity and simply say that I would be working in the county for the next six months and that I was offering free help, in confidence, for anyone with an idea for a new business or anyone willing to expand an existing one.

51

During my first week, a local committee was formed and I explained to them the concept of facilitation. I asked them to introduce me to as many people as possible and was invited to all the local social clubs, had bottomless cups of coffee with local people, and found my first ten clients in that first week. (I have to say that the Lincoln County Local Enterprise Committee became, and still is, the most extraordinary supporter and advocate of the approach. Not only were they prepared to go along with what was absolutely novel to them; they became, for a time, the sole "custodians" of the facilitation philosophy in the U.S.A. and they guarded it as if their lives depended upon it!)

After six months I had 40 clients, from which four were in an advanced stage of business preparation.

Before I left I was asked to train twelve "would-be" facilitators, including one to take over my position in Lincoln County. So Vince Robinson became the first American facilitator. In April 1989, I left Vince with a list of clients and some words of encouragement and headed back to Australia.

I didn't hear from him for the next four years until I was invited to return to Minnesota. Then I heard Vince's story.

He had spent four days in a training course trying to understand what Brian (who had joined me for the training course) and I were talking about. Then, after all of 20 minutes with me to discuss Lincoln County's enterprises, he had been left alone to make it happen.

He soon discovered, and he likes to emphasize it, that his Masters degree in Business Administration (MBA), instead of preparing him for his task of facilitating enterprises, hindered him: "What good is it to know everything about leveraged buyouts if your client cannot raise $500 to advertise her new shop?" It took Vince several months to fully appreciate the difference between a business advisor and an enterprise facilitator. In his own words, things started to improve when he realized that some of his clients grappled with problems which were not "business problems" but rather personal ones related to their own motivation, needs, and fears. The great majority of his clients, as is always the case with enterprise facilitators, were not in business yet. His clients wanted to start a business but were encountering the problems that doing something new often brings.

Finally, Vince's total commitment to his work and his dedication to rural people and rural values made him rethink his approach and shift his focus from the business aspects to the personal needs (at least in the very first stages of the project). So, for instance, he would don his work clothes, take his toolbox, and help fit out a shop in time for the opening of the tourist season.

Vince had since developed a reputation as someone who truly cares about his clients, someone who believes that Lincoln County is as good a place to do what you love doing as anywhere else. The results have certainly proved him right.

On the 5th of May 1994, the *Star Tribune*, the leading newspaper in Minnesota, included a long article by Tony Carideo entitled "Lincoln's State of Mind." Carideo wrote:

> As long as we're thinking about our borders, let us hope that distant Lincoln County—right on the Minnesota-South Dakota border—is able to hold onto the sense of place and importance that it evidently has developed over the past few years, thanks in part to Ernesto Sirolli and Vince Robinson. The article went on to say: In a six month stay in Lincoln County in 1989, Sirolli helped set up the program and trained Robinson and others how to nurture new businesses and help existing ones grow. Since then, Robinson and Lincoln County—whose scant population of 6,800 has the oldest average age in the state—have helped start 30 businesses and assisted 127 existing ones. These efforts have retained 55 jobs and created 71 jobs, a good sized number considering that the county's work force totals only 3,000.

What a surprise it was to go back to Lincoln County after four years! Another landscape—something never seen or imagined: Lincoln County in SUMMER!

Green fields and blue lakes and infinite sky. Even the barren hills of Buffalo Ridge had been transformed—covered by a swarm of windmills, producing electricity out of their barren and windswept flanks. I couldn't stop myself laughing at the vision of so many windmills. I thought of the local people as many Don Quixotes who, instead of fighting the windmills, erected them to demonstrate that you can make something out of nothing, out of the poorest land and the most desolate landscape.

Don and Sandy, whom I'd met on my first visit there, had been dreaming about setting up a fish farm. They greeted me from the newly erected veranda of their "Fish-Your-Own-Trout" Tourist Farm. I gave them a big hug because I could hardly speak! I thought of the times when, during the bleakest winter days, I would sit in their kitchen warming up with a cup of coffee, going through plans which looked impossible to realize. I could only talk with Don late in the day because he worked all night, miles from home, cleaning supermarkets. Here they were, four years on, opening their own fish farm and looking so different from how I remembered them—smiling and proud.

Traveling across the Midwest in the company of Vince, as we addressed yet another rural community, we often reminisced about the time when I had been sent to Lincoln County and we blessed Keigh Hubble for having thought of it. Because, as Vince says, "If it works in Lincoln County ... it will work anywhere!"

South Dakota

It was on the occasion of one of my many public presentations that Vince and I crossed the border to address a meeting in Madison, South Dakota.

That meeting was the catalyst for a series of events which led to an invitation to return to the U.S.A. in 1995 and to my subsequently taking up residence here. Among the civic leaders and economic practitioners who I met in Madison, a particular group had been involved in an application for a new federal fund for community development. A presidential initiative, the EC/EZ (Enterprise Community/Enterprise Zones) scheme provided a once-only grant to rural and inner-city communities identified as at risk. In the case of South Dakota, it was deemed that an area straddling two counties, in the middle of the state, would qualify for the grant as 35% of the population had an income below the national poverty line. When it was announced that the application had been successful, I was invited to spend six months with the newly formed Board of Beadle and Spink Counties Enterprise Community. Armed with a fellowship from South Dakota State University, I left Australia for yet another tough assignment: a rural community of 4,200 people, with 35% living below the poverty line, in an area of 1,000 square miles in the middle of the Prairies.

Our prior experience in Lincoln County served my family well. This time my wife and daughter were prepared for a prairie winter. Our concerns in that first year were only for our newly built Australian home which, as it happened, was in the hands of the "tenants from hell!"

Work was, as usual, exhilarating. There is nothing like being a total stranger in a new community and having to measure yourself with your own beliefs and fears. Even experienced skydivers get a thrill every time the parachute opens! We Enterprise Facilitators get a thrill every time our "parachute" opens and we prove to ourselves, yet again, that we can help someone to go all the way from having a dream to realizing it.

The frozen welder

Rollie Watson had a problem. None of the modern agricultural machinery he was asked to repair seemed to fit through the door of the 1940s workshop he had recently leased! "I have plenty of work," he told me during our first visit, "but I can only last half an hour in the open before I freeze." He wasn't joking either, since sub-zero temperatures in the plains are the stuff rural legends are made of.

He needed a bigger building or he would have to give up the business. Strong, sharp, in his forties, with eight children from two marriages, and finances to match his family situation, Rollie Watson had reached the limit of what he could do by himself.

After losing his cattle farm, Rollie had settled in Yale, population 120, where he had worked for three years maintaining and repairing farming equipment for a wealthy local producer. His life had been reasonably uneventful until the manager of the local grain elevator cooperative had strongly urged him to reopen the old welding workshop, the closure of which had condemned local farmers to a seventy-mile trip to the nearest repair shop. Asking price for the cement brick building was a modest $5,000, but even that price was too much for Rollie, and he was convinced to take the plunge only after a five-year lease/purchase plan was offered to him.

The patronage of the new venture was instant and overwhelming. The town had a small population, but the cooperative had 700 members, of which 450 were active farmers. They gave Rollie at least $100,000 worth of work in the first five months of operation. Rollie could only manage half of it and then wait for the thaw to do the rest...and he was very unhappy about that! Mostly he blamed the banks for not lending him money based on his earning potential. "Security I don't have," he readily agreed, "but couldn't the banks look at the earning potential and track record of this enterprise?"

55

He knew the question was rhetorical, though. He was no fool and agreed to meet with me because he understood exactly the predicament he was in. One of my board members, a county commissioner who had lived in Yale, organized our meeting in the hope that I could help Rollie as he believed that Rollie was doing a great job for the local farmers.

Two things struck me at that first meeting: Rollie's passion for his work and his truly remarkable fabricating skills. This was a guy who loved what he was doing and was frustrated by having so little with which to do so much.

During the following weeks, we revisited all the local banks (six) and special rural funds (one) and came to the conclusion that Rollie was $35,000 short of securing a $55,000 building loan. This latter figure was the least expensive quote Rollie could find after he had decided to partially build the new building himself. Still, how to get the security?

"Could you get a partner interested in joining you?" My question was answered with a "Maybe." Then, within a few days, an invitation came for me to meet "Cowboy." "Cowboy" had been described to me before; meeting him confirmed my suspicions...here was a guy who, during his vacations, would come to visit Rollie and for fun would don his leathers and weld from 7 a.m. to 7 p.m.! "I have so much fun," he told me,"the time goes so quickly." A supervising foreman in a large packing plant in Wisconsin, Cowboy missed the urgency and the challenge of working in a small business. He admired Rollie, and Rollie could not speak highly enough of his friend who had all the imaginable welding certificates and who had been supervising dozens of people for many years.

It did not take much for a deal to be struck and for the friends and their wives to become partners; unfortunately, even combining their equipment and inventory, they still came short of $20,000 to secure a bank loan. We had to develop a different strategy and decided that the quality of the people involved in the new company, their track record, and their client base were enough to seek investment funding from one or more private investors.

We assembled a team: Production, Marketing, and Financial Management, and produced the best business plan we were capable of. Under production we listed Rollie and Cowboy's skills and qualifications and attached a full inventory of equipment owned by the company and color photocopies of finished work with testimonials from satisfied clients. With the marketing documents, we included a letter from an implements marketing organization willing to represent some of the company's products. We attached a list of 120 recent clients and a South Dakota government survey which indicated that every farmer in the state spends an average $6,500 per year on maintenance of agricultural equipment. We highlighted, in the business plan, the fact that the 450 local farmers represented a potential captive market worth $2,925,000 per year.

The chairman of our Enterprise Facilitation board, a well-respected CPA who graciously donated his time to this local enterprise, prepared financial projections. The final business plan looked as if we were raising a million dollars instead of the hoped-for $25,000.

The first person to see this business plan was Dennis Wiese the president of the South Dakota Farmer's Union who, suitably impressed, requested that a presentation be made to his board, which historically had never invested in a venture like this one. After the presentation, the board, probably reassured by the fact that the CPA involved was also their auditor (!), took the plunge and offered the partners to invest $25,000, on favorable commercial terms. On the strength of their capital injection, a local bank lent another $30,000 to the company.

That same evening Rollie called me and asked me to come visit him; he had to show me something urgently, something he was kicking himself for not having seen sooner ....

As soon as I arrived, Rollie took me behind his old workshop and pointed to the Quonset hut across the highway, partially obscured by a thicket of trees. "It is the old school gymnasium," he told me. "It has been empty for 25 years and is one-third bigger than the building we plan to build." He continued to tell me that it had just dawned on him that the building could be easily converted and that he was still astonished at how something so obvious could have escaped him.

We then walked across the road and literally bought the building for $13,000 cash. The partners spent $30,000 refurbishing the building and fitting the gymnasium with a massive hydraulic door of their make. When the bank assessor came to appraise the building he awarded the property a value of

$90,000. The old workshop became the spraying booth and Rollie and Cowboy were on their way. Within two years, they employed 27 people and had orders to the value of $90,000 per month.

Finally, one of their major clients, a Mennonite community, asked them to set up a very large manufacturing plant in a nearby town and Rollie and Cowboy were convinced to supervise and manage one of the largest manufacturing plants in the region.

The difference between Rollie's survival and the creation of many jobs in the area was, amazingly, $25,000. This is often the case in rural and inner-city facilitation. The difference between success and failure rests often on ensuring a relatively small amount of start-up money, but it is precisely this first investment money that is the hardest to get and requires the best skills a facilitator has.

Victor

Working in Yale had spoiled me; my next client came from Victor, South Dakota, population twelve people!

Gene Paulson told me, with nostalgia, that once Victor's population had been fourteen! He was probably making fun of me, but doubting him would have been unwise.

You had to be careful with this guy; he had invited me to a meeting with a group of Japanese buyers. He told me the name of the Japanese company they represented, and it was very hard for me to imagine such people traveling around the world to Victor. After all, the company in question has an annual budget the size of that of a small European country and Victor ... well you really have to know where to look, otherwise you miss it!

That particular night, however, the supper club in Victor was full, and around a long table sat, on one side, organic farmers in their plaid shirts and John Deere caps, and on the other, seven very well dressed Japanese businessmen in suits and loafers! Gene had not been telling tales; the Japanese not only were there, they meant business and so did the farmers. As the organizer of a group of organic farmers, Gene had been cleaning and exporting organic grains for many years.

He had approached me wanting to talk about the farm situation, rural America, the international trade, his company, and where to go next.

What Gene and his friends had done was fantastic. They had bought and retrofitted a small grain elevator using what looked like scrap metal and found objects; the place didn't look like much but surely it worked! They screened and packed containers of organic produce for export and had gained the respect of very important companies not only in Japan but also in Europe. From a very efficient office, Gene and his wife were sifting through stacks of mostly export orders.

The complexities and the demands of both farmers and buyers required speed and flexibility in filling orders—something hard to achieve for a small elevator with a limited holding capacity and with screening equipment which required complete cleaning every time a new grain was processed. Gene had to make some important decisions: "To grow or not to grow and at what price? Should we build here or find an existing facility?" He kept asking my advice but did not really need the answer; what he needed was a soul mate who could rebound his passion and listen to his dreams with undivided attention, ready to jump into action as soon as he made up his mind.

He called me one day; he wanted me to look over an empty grain elevator. On the drive there he kept talking about how big the place was. "Too big for us," he said, "and too old. It is also in poor condition and probably too expensive."

We inspected the site the way you view a once beautiful classic car. You don't want to like it! "No," you keep repeating to yourself, "too rusty, too hard to fix." Yet ... the place had 500,000 bushels of storage capacity, 270 separate overhead bins, gravitation tables, and a train loading bay with its own set of near-functioning scales! I could see Gene saying no with his mouth, but the place was, to a farmer, trucker, and entrepreneur ... irresistible.

From a marketing point of view, the idea of 500,000 bushels of clean organic grains in 270 separate bins had enormous appeal, and we drove away that day trying not to show how excited we were. Months of negotiations, meetings, and red tape followed, but Gene finally moved in and had the plant sparkling clean for the harvest of 1998.

Organic farmers are calling him now, and there is a stir of excitement around Victor. Could it be that many more farmers, led by Gene, will learn to work together and market their commodities or even finished products? Maybe not, but who can say? After all the name Victor, in Latin, means "He who wins."

To stay or not to stay?

After six months, the first success story had appeared in the local press and a color insert told the story of Rollie and Cowboy. It was all there: their hopes, their appreciation for the help received, even their pictures (with them wearing welding helmets!). The president of South Dakota Faurmers Union was interested in doing more." Could we set up a center for rural development? Could we do this nationally?"

For my family, this meant committing ourselves to a new life in North America, selling our home, putting our worldly goods into storage, and starting over again with school, friends, and colleagues. When a large electric utility in Minnesota let us know that they were also interested in starting a project, we decided to stay. We moved to Sioux Falls to be able to commute between both locations and also because in Sioux Falls there was Zambroz, a wonderful coffee bar making real espresso!

The coldest winter in 100 years!

We had heard about it but we had never seen it. In 1989, our first Midwest winter, we were told to carry in our emergency road kit some red cloth to tie onto the car aerial in case we got trapped in a blizzard. We shook our heads in disbelief. In 1997, we actually saw quite a few red cloth ties sticking out of snow banks on the highway between Sioux Falls and Minneapolis.

The commute was a five-hour drive, but became longer after I destroyed the first car in a rendition of "Swan Lake" on black ice and started to drive real slow! Except for the commute, work went well and we set the basis for future work with funding from two foundations. The first aimed to establish Enterprise Facilitation projects in South Dakota and southwest Minnesota, and the other to set up projects in Dakota County, a booming suburban area south of the twin cities of Minneapolis and St. Paul.

The Badlands and other projects

If you travel due west from Sioux Falls, follow the signs to Wall Drugs. Once in Wall, turn left and let history grab you—you are in the Badlands. Gone are the lines of tourists and the gimmicky signs advertising free water;

now you are confronted with a landscape that is both eerie and splendid. Without warning, the Plains vanish and a lunar landscape of eroded peaks and canyons appears. The change is so sudden after hundreds of miles of prairies that it shocks the traveler who pulls over to the verge, steps out, and silently stares. People are quiet in the Badlands, including the children who are strangely subdued as if they were in church or on sacred ground. Wounded Knee is only miles away . . . even an Italian like me knows the story and can feel the sorrow that haunts the place.

Eight different counties had come together to establish an Enterprise Facilitation project in an area of 12,500 square miles, with a population of 25,000 people. This large number of organizations had been coordinated by the excellent staff of the local RC&D (Regional Conservation and Development), a federally funded initiative. Civic leaders and personnel from counties, towns, local banks, and the Rosebud Native American Reservation had attended a number of presentations on Enterprise Facilitation and had become interested in pursuing the approach.

The Northwest Area Foundation provided funding for several pilot projects, and the Badlands Enterprise Facilitation project was created. A very large board was formed and trained (twenty-one volunteers were needed to provide outreach in the eight counties), and an Enterprise Facilitator was employed.

Nancy Larsen had just relocated to Martin, population 1,551, when she took her position as Enterprise Facilitator on June 1st, 1997. Contrary to some of the other Enterprise Facilitators, who experienced a slower start, she had to hit the ground running. The main reason for her busy start was the fact that it had taken her local steering committee over a year to secure project funding. During that period, the committee had started to spread the word that a free, confidential service would soon be available to local entrepreneurs. People had responded, and Nancy had 20 clients waiting for her!

Nancy's first success was to assist a young couple to reopen the old movie theatre in Martin. With help from Nancy, they were able to secure a loan and establish the theatre as one of the very few entertainment venues in the area.

After 15 months, she has been approached by 116 local entrepreneurs and has 71 active files which to date have assisted in the creation of 48 new jobs. An impressive figure for one of the most impoverished and isolated regions of the United States. Per capita income in this area is $6,675 per year, including Shannon County, which was ranked as the third poorest county in the U.S.A. with an average annual income of $3,400 per person.

Nancy says her job is not for the faint of heart. If this is the case, then the people who offered her the job were very smart because they understood how brave and resolute she is.

David Lambert, the Enterprise Facilitator in Parker, South Dakota, was not as busy as Nancy to start with but soon caught up. His steering committee is comprised of people from one county and two cities. The start-up of this project followed traditional lines: board's outreach leading to introductions resulting in clients' referrals and first successes.

Dr. Chicoine, a local champion of Enterprise Facilitation who had then joined the board, took particular satisfaction in their early results. Meeting with a Canadian delegation only two months after David had begun as an Enterprise Facilitator, he remarked that he had been involved in traditional economic development for twenty years and that during that time he had been able to "attract" only one company employing twenty people to the area. He made the comment that "since David has been here, he has worked with twenty-one entrepreneurs and it seems that we are doing more now without initiating anything than when we were trying really hard!"

By October 1998, David was well established and recognized with 127 clients of whom 67 were actively involved in starting new enterprises.

Hastings, Minnesota

A pretty historic town of 18,000 people on the Mississippi River, Hastings has retained its Main Street pretty much intact. The lovingly restored Old Town Hall dominates the business district where grand old buildings have been put to good use, including some which have been transformed into very beautiful bed-and-breakfasts catering to travelers and weekenders from the nearby Minneapolis-St. Paul area.

Championed by the indefatigable La Donna Boyd of Dakota Electric, Enterprise Facilitation was embraced by a group of civic leaders and sponsors in Dakota County. They secured funding from the McKnight Foundation and then made an intense effort to raise local matching funds.

62

The city council, the hospital administration, the industrial development committee, the Chamber of Commerce, and a local bank all joined in. The county became the fiscal agent, and Ron Toppin, a local retailer, was appointed to the position of Enterprise Facilitator.

Ron's patience, generosity, and personal understanding of small business guaranteed his success. After 16 months, Ron had assisted 102 new clients, established 10 new businesses, and assisted with the expansion of 12 others, contributing to the creation of 42 jobs in the community.

The urban challenge

Vince Robinson, of Lincoln County fame, was invited to address a conference in Minneapolis in 1996. He spoke with his usual forceful blend of love for rural communities and contempt for urban solutions to rural problems. During his presentation, he displayed the following table:

Lincoln County, Minnesota, approximate population 6,800	
Total projects	351
Successful business start-ups	55
Business expansions	61
Years in operation	6
New jobs created	180
Average cost per job over six years	$1,833
New wages form assisted projects	$2.0 million annually

Representing Hennepin County at the conference were John McLaughlin and Larry Blackstead who were intrigued by Vince's experience in one of the poorest counties in the state. They inquired about urban applications of Enterprise Facilitation and, having been introduced to them, we were soon discussing some of the issues confronting inner-city communities in America.

Hennepin County is one of the largest counties in the U.S.A., encompassing the city of Minneapolis. That city, like many large American cities, has seen a mass migration of the middle classes away from the heart of town to newer suburbs. What has been left behind has become a wasteland of decaying buildings, boarded-up businesses, and vacant lots. This has become a perfect habitat for the transient, the poor, and those who prey on them.

Cities all over the world develop a variety of strategies to fight urban decay — mostly they throw money at the problem! Many millions of dollars are spent annually by city administrations attempting to regentrify neighborhoods, in much the same manner plastic surgeons attempt to return people to their youth! Often entire city blocks are torn down; empty car lots and modern strip malls replace once beautiful inner-city areas, where people were able to live, work, go to school, and shop — imagine that!

Concerned, John and Larry were looking at the inner-city situation and wondering whether more could be done to restore a sense of pride and place among its residents. "There must be a better way," John remarked.

My experience in small rural communities had prepared me for bringing some hope and resources to people who, wrongly, felt inadequate to tackle the economic challenges facing them. But 60% unemployment? I had never seen that in the country. Even poverty in the city looks different: rental apartments, fast food containers strewn all over the place, televisions blaring, the gas disconnected, and a sensation of danger everywhere. What can be done here? Is this a real community or a refugee camp?

My proposed course of action was to ascertain the existence of true community leadership by introducing the concept of Enterprise Facilitation to as many communities as possible and seeing what would happen. Leave it to the locals to decide whether they would endorse and support the model or not.

Hennepin County agreed to commission a series of community presentations on the understanding that it could not and would not establish Enterprise Facilitation programs as a top-down initiative.

The immediate difference between rural and inner city became obvious after the first few meetings. In the country there are too few resources, in the city there are too many! In one neighborhood, population 60,000, there were an estimated 200 nonprofit organizations trying to assist residents! You can imagine the initial reaction of local activists to yet another program! Many held the attitude that they were already doing what we suggested and pointed at a number of small business services in

Minneapolis such as entrepreneurial management courses microenterprise lending, small business incubation, mentoring services, etc.

What could Enterprise Facilitation offer that was not already there?

Too much, too little

It took a few months before a number of community leaders started to realize some of the peculiar strengths of Enterprise Facilitation. With great generosity of spirit, a dozen community development practitioners made sincere attempts to understand both the philosophy and the practice of Enterprise Facilitation and gave me a better understanding of the issues which confronted them.

Nearly all the nonprofit agencies working in local communities had economic development, job creation, or entrepreneurial support in their mission statements. It seemed, however, that they had all been established with a major focus in mind other than one-on-one work with entrepreneurs. They were involved in housing rehabilitation, microloan lending, training, delivery of welfare services, literacy programs, neighborhood beautification, etc.

When we started to analyze our roles, it seemed that they all wanted to do Enterprise Facilitation, but did not have the time or the full-time personnel to do so. On top of that, those agencies which linked their advisory role to other activities such as training, lending, etc. experienced all sorts of problems. In the area of training, for instance, the programs offered in the city emphasized the importance, for the entrepreneurs, of learning all facets of the business. The course offered required the client to complete a business plan before he or she could apply for funding or assistance.

Enterprise Facilitation, however, teaches that nobody on earth is equally passionate about producing a product, marketing it, and keeping good financial records. The clients are required to analyze what their passion is and to honestly assess what it is that they are the least capable of doing. Next, with the facilitator's assistance if necessary, they have to form the management team capable of establishing and operating the business. It is the *team* that writes the business plan, not the individual entrepreneur. Enterprise Facilitation actually discourages individuals from writing a business plan in isolation because people only do well what they love doing, and in business this is not enough.

Our experience resonated with many civic leaders and practitioners in Hennepin County, who had observed clients unable to run a business even though they had successfully completed a business plan.

Another major difference between Enterprise Facilitation and existing programs was in the area of lending. Enterprise Facilitators never lend money to clients because they know that a good proposal, with a good management team in place, will find either institutional lenders or private investors to back it. After all, there is far more money around than good projects to lend it to!

Some of the practitioners involved in microloan lending appreciated the wisdom of teaching team-management practices instead of lending money to would-be entrepreneurs. As lenders, they had experienced the problem of trying to "pick winners." They knew of the agony of having to reject applicants, sometimes after they had completed weeks of prescribed training. They were aware of the conflict between lending and advising the same clients on how to secure a loan. They had become involved in trying to rescue poorly managed businesses by spending hundreds of hours with one client and had experienced public criticism when they had to shut down delinquent businesses.

They started to see how Enterprise Facilitation would complement existing initiatives. An Enterprise Facilitator could prepare clients to use the programs and resources available in the community, making the work of lenders, trainers, and other service providers much easier and more productive.

The parallel between the family physician and the specialist came to mind. Would a community be better or worse without family physicians? What would be the result of health care being only provided by specialists with patients having to guess whom to consult? An established Enterprise Facilitator will see between 150 and 200 clients per year and will be able to refer them to the appropriate "specialist," who can then provide finance, training, locations, and an endless supply of technical advice.

By April 1998, some 150 community lenders, economic development specialists, and a host of interested parties joined together to provide management funds, in-kind contributions, and resources to establish six Enterprise Facilitation projects within Hennepin County. Four were neighborhood-based and two were established in cities within the greater metropolitan area of Minneapolis.

Within months of starting, by October 1998, the six projects had had the following impact:

- Board Members had introduced the facilitators to 500 residents;
- Following introductions, Enterprise Facilitators had been contacted by 271 interested parties;
- 87 of them had become clients and were actively pursuing their enterprise plans.

In light of the novelty of the projects, it seems safe to assume that this first metropolitan Enterprise Facilitation program is going to produce results comparable to the best rural projects. Without a doubt, urban Enterprise Facilitators will experience the same demand for their services as their rural colleagues.

City logistics

One of the advantages to starting projects in close geographic proximity has been the camaraderie between the Enterprise Facilitators. They meet informally, usually patronizing local cafés, sharing experiences, and providing valuable support to each other.

In terms of funding, it has been possible for civic leaders to approach the same funding sources and to leverage the good will created by one project for the benefit of others. A typical example was project funding obtained from the Norwest Bank (now Wells Fargo) Foundation and Hennepin County, which eventually became involved in matching 25% for each project, the remaining 75% being raised and managed locally.

Canada

Without Yvonne Fizer, it would have taken years to introduce Enterprise Facilitation to Canada. A home-based business advisor with the Alberta provincial government, Yvonne had experienced the reality of entrepreneurship. She had seen large numbers of people opting for self-employment not only on financial grounds, but also for quality-of-life reasons. Young parents were asking themselves: "Should we pay for child care and commute every day, or should we find a way to start working from home?"

Enterprise Facilitation made sense to Yvonne who had seen the struggle of home-based entrepreneurs, and she became a "champion" of the approach. Having heard a presentation in the U.S.A., she organized with Barbara Moat, a well-known Canadian entrepreneur, a tour of Alberta and British Columbia to introduce the concept. The initial response was **67** positive, but things took on a different dimension when Yvonne, faced with yet another downsizing of the provincial government department she worked for, secured a severance package and set herself free.

Yvonne attended a five-day Enterprise Facilitator training course and then announced that she wanted to establish an office in Canada. Since that start in early 1997, she has organized ten training courses, established three Enterprise Facilitation projects, and introduced at least 4,000 people to the concept through conferences and community speaking. She has also inspired several passionate individuals to become involved in championing our work.

Among them is Bob Williams who held the portfolio of Minister for Finance in the provincial government of British Columbia in the seventies. Since then, he has been a board member of VanCity Credit and Savings Union, the largest credit union in Canada, and in 1998 he chaired the VanCity Regional Development Corporation, an organization which was looking for innovative ways to use credit for the enhancement of civic society.

Meeting Bob was like looking out of a window after having been in a dark room! VanCity was doing both innovative and good work like financing car pool cooperatives and establishing financial trusts for families of the intellectually impaired. Remarkably, it was doing so in a financial win-win situation, leaving both the community and the credit union in better shape.

Not only did Bob Williams become a champion of Enterprise Facilitation he has been, and continues to be, an inspiration in developing social technology to foster civic society.

Camrose, Stettler, and New Westminster

Camrose, the first project in Canada, had Randy Niven as its champion. Randy was working for the provincial government advising the local administration on improved ways to deliver government programs. He was keen to set up a pilot project as a demonstration of Enterprise Facilitation and managed to secure a federal grant for the Camrose area, a rural county located halfway between Edmonton and Calgary in Alberta.

In January 1998, a local steering committee was formed and trained, and the work began. By October 1998, Betty Deck, the Enterprise Facilitator, had seen sixty people and had more than twenty active clients in various stages of business.

The challenge for this new project will be to attract local sponsors and local government support after the initial grant is exhausted. To be truly successful, the project will have to demonstrate its worth to local leaders who will then incorporate Enterprise Facilitation in their economic development strategies. Enterprise Facilitation can be demonstrated to a community but its long-term success has to rely on local ownership and support.

The local government in Stettler, a rural community not far from Camrose, made the decision that Enterprise Facilitation would be funded by local rates. Every ratepayer was taxed an additional $16 per year and every business an additional $76.

Naturally this has put the Enterprise Facilitator in Stettler, Gaye Stewart, the spotlight. Her job has the potential of becoming a political football, since every challenger for council positions may attack Enterprise Facilitation on fiscal grounds no matter what results it may bring. Because Enterprise Facilitation projects require a minimum of two years to generate sizeable results, we recommend that funding be raised and be guaranteed for a minimum of 24 months. We also strongly advocate funding partnerships, that is with local, provincial, state, or federal governments; financial institutions; foundations; corporations; utilities; and private citizens.

With rural projects, we recommend participation by every city within a county or shire, so that ownership in the project is shared and the financial exposure for all participants minimized.

A typical project could have a budget of $80,000 per year; of this $20,000 may be in-kind contributions from local governments, banks, or Chambers of Commerce. This could take the form of office space, telephone, computer, receptionist services, etc. Of the remaining $60,000, 25% could come from the shire or government, 25% from all cities in the local government area on a pro rata share based on population size, 25% from federal sources or foundations, and the final 25% from corporate interests in the region. A combination of many investors provides two guarantees:

- one funding agency does not have total fiscal control of the project to politicize it;
- through the incentive of shared ownership many partners will have an interest in seeing the project succeed.

These first Canadian Enterprise Facilitation projects demonstrate diverse funding arrangements but make it possible for one funding agency to determine whether to terminate or continue the project; this places the Enterprise Facilitator under pressure to deliver quick results.

After only a few months of work, Gaye and Betty, our first two full-time community Enterprise Facilitators in Canada, have demonstrated their worth and have received superb testimonials from the clients that they have already helped. This notwithstanding, the next year will illustrate whether having multiple funding partners is as essential in Canada as in other parts of the world.

In terms of funding strategy, New Westminster, one of the oldest cities in British Columbia, is closer to our ideal model. Local and federal funding has been raised, VanCity Credit Union is a major sponsor, and so is the local Community Skill Center, which has provided leadership and coordination.

At the time of writing (October 1998), the local management board had been inducted and trained and ads had been placed to recruit the first Enterprise Facilitator in British Columbia.

New West, as the city is often referred to, has a population of 60,000 people and is a community which engenders great passion among its residents. Our hope is for the right person to claim the position of Enterprise Facilitator, someone who can transform local resolve into tangible results.

The big Australian

Ask any Australian who the "big" Australian is and you will hear the story of Broken Hill Propriety (BHP), the biggest Australian Corporation for the past one hundred years.

Broken Hill was the legendary rich mine discovered last century in the outback of New South Wales. The corporation that managed its wealth has been an Australian icon for five generations. Today BHP is a diversified conglomerate operating worldwide. BHP is a mining giant, are oil company, and the foremost steel maker in Australia.

It was at the beginning of this century that BHP built a steel mill at the port of Newcastle in New South Wales. The reasons for picking Newcastle were the same that prompted the early colonial power to establish a settlement there: huge coalfields and a beautiful deep harbor for shipping the black gold to nearby Sydney.

In the fifties, the Newcastle Steel Mill became a huge complex employing more than 20,000 workers and transforming Newcastle from Coal City to Steel City. For decades, Newcastle's ethos has been shaped by the steel works, which have influenced everything from the name of the local football team (The Knights), to theatre productions (Steel City).

When, in 1997, BHP announced the closure of its Newcastle steel mill, the city, then the region, then the nation, went into shock. "This cannot be" was the common reaction from people whose grandparents had moved from Europe to work at the steel mill. The mill was the reason for many to migrate to Australia; it has been a veritable institution which had provided a passport to a new life and the security necessary to buy a house, build a community, and face the future with confidence.

Yet by the mid-eighties, the actual size and importance of the steel mill had declined. Two thousand workers remained, and although sizeable, their lay-off was considered not to have too much effect on the city of 120,000 people and the surrounding Hunter Valley with a population of 500,000 people.

The shock was more psychological than real, but it did not stop local civic leaders from worrying. They understood how potentially dangerous negative sentiments can be for the economy. If panic hits a market, no matter how unfounded the cause may be, the consequences may be dire.

BHP announced the closure of the mill just before a week-long international conference, hosted by Newcastle City Council, dealing with "Pathways to Sustainability"! This conference, a follow-up to the Rio Summit, had been organized in cooperation with the United Nations and was meant to address the role that local governments play in the pursuit of sustainability.

A special panel of speakers was quickly convened to discuss the implications of the steel mill closure. In that context, I met BHP's local Public Affairs Director and was introduced to the strategies that BHP and interested parties had been developing to respond to the long-term concerns of workers, the community, and the Australian public.

The key to BHP's strategy was consultation and transparency. The company announced the closure of the mill two years prior to the closing, a very different approach from corporations that post a sign on the gate after they have chained it shut.

As a first priority, BHP had taken care of its workers by negotiating generous and comprehensive redundancy packages with the trade unions. It did so based on civic but also sound economic judgement since every day lost to industrial dispute could have cost the company more than a million dollars in profit. Industrial unrest also could have spread around Australia and hit have the company both nationally and internationally.

Then BHP started to look at the community. It made the decision to become involved in providing leadership and participating in a number of initiatives, which, if successful, could provide the town with a long-term economic boost. BHP proposed the creation of an eco-industrial park on an old industrial site they owned. (An eco-industrial park meets Environmental Protection Agency standards and pre-negotiates what kind of industries may locate there.) The site, renamed "Steel River," became the focus for extensive and often heated community involvement and consultation. Months of work went into the creation of this first eco-industrial park in Australia. The exercise successfully mobilized civic leadership to engage in a positive process of building the future of their community. The corporations, the unions, all levels of government, civic leaders, and a host of local agencies had come together with one aim in mind: to make Newcastle a thriving city of opportunities for generations to come. Working together, former antagonists discovered the power of solidarity and achieved results that would have eluded them individually.

"Steel River" became the first eco-industrial park in Australia to be granted federal import tax concessions under a manufacture-in-bond statute, which was drafted in Newcastle. (Manufacturing in bond allows goods to be imported, processed, and exported without import duties being levied.) The park also developed a fast-track, 21-day guaranteed development approval process by negotiating with the many regulatory agencies involved. (Guaranteed development approval means that all the bureaucratic red tape is spelled out to the developer in one document. If the developer meets the requirements, a development permit is issued in 21 days.) The bureaucracies, according to those involved in the negotiations, would not have been as accommodating without strong local leadership.

Strong leadership had also resulted in a $20 million fund being established by BHP as well as state and federal governments to attract new business to the region. The "BHP Trust" had immediately commissioned a study of industrial clusters to look at the potential for developing synergies among local companies. The overall strategy put in place by civic leaders took care of the "big end" of the town, that is, the large- and medium-size existing companies. They were provided financial incentives, land tax concessions, fast-track development approvals, and technical expertise for the development of specialized industrial clusters.

What was missing, in my view, was a strategy to enhance and capitalize on local entrepreneurship, not only in the city of Newcastle, but the greater region of the Hunter Valley.

After my presentation to the "Pathways to Sustainability" conference, I met with BHP and the Lord Mayor of Newcastle. The discussion centered on the opportunities that the steel mill closure could bring Newcastle and the Hunter Valley, if only civic energy could be focused on creating physical and social infrastructure to ride the wave of change. Civic leadership, in my view, had the chance of becoming directly involved in generating wealth by transforming Newcastle, and the Hunter Valley, into a region that facilitated entrepreneurship. They could easily replace the lost 2,000 jobs at the steel mill if they could offer to the laid-off workers, and the region's residents, caring and professional advice to start their own enterprises.

Apparently, there were already 300 BHP workers who had expressed an interest in starting their own businesses and BHP thought that Enterprise Facilitation could become an additional tool in its quest for a peaceful and considerate outcome to the mill's closure. The Lord Mayor of Newcastle also expressed his interest in Enterprise Facilitation but more from a social perspective, that is, to make sure that the people of Newcastle would not become victims of the massive economic restructuring taking place.

Both BHP and the City of Newcastle asked that an extensive community consultation process be undertaken to ascertain the interest of the region's leadership. If endorsed, Enterprise Facilitation would become the third leg of an integrated regional development strategy to cater to both the "big end" and the "small end" of town and to enable the Hunter Valley to offer quality resources to all entrepreneurs, from rural start-ups to multinational corporations.

In September 1997, the consultative process began. Local government, unions, development agencies, and a variety of interested parties through-out the Hunter Valley expressed strong support for Enterprise Facilitation. As a result, the BHP Trust, composed of a company representative, the NSW state government, and the Australian federal government commissioned the establishment of up to ten Enterprise Facilitation projects in the Hunter Valley.

By June of 1998, sixteen local partnerships had expressed their intention to establish an Enterprise Facilitation project in their community. Such groups had offered cash and contributions in-kind and volunteered resources to manage the projects. By November 1998, a funding strategy was developed which aimed at matching local resources with corporate funding and creating a foundation with 125% tax deductible status.

At the time of going to print, three of Australia's largest corporations had indicated their willingness to receive formal funding submissions. The work of establishing the structure for the foundation tax status was underway, with fund-raising to start in 1999.

If successful, Newcastle and the Hunter Region will become a model of how local leadership can transform a potentially demoralizing event into an opportunity for rejuvenation. It could be a working model for a partnership among private and public sectors to manage change utilizing a social technology — Enterprise Facilitation — which beautifully complements top-down initiatives by mobilizing and capturing local energy and talent.

PART TWO

THE PRESENT

8. ON FACILITATION

THIS SECTION OF THE BOOK IS THE "HANDS-ON," PRACTICAL PART. IT describes how to facilitate and what to do when you are appointed to work in a community — the "tricks of the trade," so to speak, and the pitfalls to avoid.

Before we embark on the practicalities, however, I would like you to read carefully the following section, which is a general introduction to facilitation. It will, I hope, make it clear why some people succeed and others don't and will hopefully prevent some heartache among those of the readers who will become involved in facilitation.

Set the sail

> "I can't myself raise the winds that might blow us, or this ship, into a better world, But I can at least put up the sail so that, when the wind comes, I can catch it."
>
> — E.F. Schumacher[1]

In 1986, the word "facilitation" was hardly ever used. At Brian Willoughby's first public meeting, he was introduced not as a "facilitator" but as a "precipitator!"

The word and the concept were new, but it didn't take long for the "bush telegraph" (the informal rural network) to spread the news that something interesting was happening in Esperance. An ABC national radio program called "Practicalities" and an SBS television documentary "Esperance — Hope for the Future" in the series Australian Mosaic also helped.

Since then, Local Enterprise Facilitation has become a recognized strategy in regional and rural development. In 1998, in Australia and New Zealand, there were an estimated 300 communities employing a full-time Enterprise Facilitator and thousands of people had been exposed to the concept.

All in all facilitation, as an idea, has been easy to sell. Who would object to the fundamental ideas that we, as individuals, are important and that we can improve our lot, create wealth, and become better people?

78

Often my listeners have witnessed success in their own communities, in the form of a committed individual who against all odds has achieved the seemingly unachievable. I can build on the examples they give and the experiences they have had. I tell my audiences that "facilitation" is based on the understanding that creativity, motivation, even genius are there amongst them often locked between the ears of their friends, relatives, spouses, even those they would never credit with having any ideas at all! "What we have to do," I say to them, "is to become available to anyone in your community who has a dream and then to help transform that dream into good work."

It is when I tell my listeners that economic development is the result of hundreds and thousands of people doing beautifully what they love doing that the questions start! "It's easy to have dreams," they say, "and to put them into practice is where we cannot share your optimism." And at this point they often come up with long lists of difficulties, obstacles, and a million and one reasons why dreamers never make it.

I then tell them about passion and skill.

On passion

> "Whenever anything is being accomplished, it is being done ...
> by a monomaniac with a mission."
>
> — P. Drucker[2]

Nothing of significance can be made without the blending of individual commitment and the physical ability to reify, that is to make real, the dream.

As far as individual commitment goes, we have to understand that psychologically healthy people grow forever — only death can stop their curiosity. To be human is to strive to become ourselves, to realize, the innate talent that we have. The psychologists call this need, the need to actualize, to make real our potential. As we saw in the chapter dedicated to Maslow's work, the need for self-actualization is our highest need, one which will haunt us no matter how otherwise "successful" we may be.

Shakespeare was not alone in admonishing us that we should be true to our call: "This above all: to thine own self be true" (Hamlet 1:3). Other cultures, other traditions also call for us to engage fully in this life and to commit ourselves to it. For instance, the Hebrew root of the verb "to sin" comes from "to miss": to miss our calling is to miss our duty towards ourselves, which is a sin. The Catholics list as one of the deadly sins: sloth. The Latin word for "sloth" is "accidia" which means the sin of failing to do in your own life what you know you ought to be doing. How many sinners do we know? How much do we sin ourselves against our own nature?

But becoming what we are is invariably difficult. We have to commit ourselves to a course that may prove to be unpopular with our peers, unfashionable among our friends, and unbecoming in the eyes of our parents. Striving for individuality is always a lonely business.

Passion is what propels us during our solitary journey. That passion manifests itself as dedication to what we are and what we do, the desire to live life fully and to return to the world the talents that have been bestowed on us. When the Lord asked the three brothers what they had done with the golden talent he had given to each of them, he was not angry at the first who had wasted it trying to invest it, nor the second who managed to make a fortune utilizing it — his wrath fell on the third brother who had buried it. For fear of living is similar to death.

A passionate life is not an easy one. Passion is not only red roses and romance, passion can also be the passion of Christ, a passion which makes you suffer but which is your personal path for self-understanding and authenticity. The common characteristic of passionate people is that they do things.

The dream of becoming a successful painter or the best shoemaker in town cannot occur without painting or making shoes. The passionate individual therefore does things: launches a business, publishes a book, designs a new product, builds a house, etc. as if the road to self-fulfillment demands that we engage both in thought and action.

Work, seen in this light, is nothing but the embodiment of our passion and, I like to tell my audiences, dreamers with passion for their dreams are a force to be reckoned with. These are potent people and not merely wishful thinkers.

But the dream is not enough and the passion useless unless you know how to make your dream visible. The dream in your head and the passion in your heart has to be complemented by the skill in your hands.

80 I then talk about skill.

On skill

> "Without skill there is no art."
> — Gregory Bateson[3]

In the sixties, creativity was the buzzword. The rejection of the authoritarian values of the previous generation included the rejection of all forms of schooling, training, and education. Pink Floyd sang: "We don't need your education, we don't need your mind control." The message was loud, psychedelic, and clear: free yourself from society's shackles, inject yourself with a mind-enhancing substance and ... create. Art was seen as freedom, as "happening," as natural as the flowering of the mind's powers.

The created objects were ugly, though, and often not very functional or durable. Sandals which fell apart in no time. Millions of brown coffee mugs which were produced by amateur potters who soon became bored with the exercise and went back to a full-time life on the dole. When the hippies left the cities to go and create Utopias near unsuspecting rural hamlets, they took with them no life-supporting skills. With few exceptions, they couldn't build a house, grow food, or organize themselves into viable self-supporting communities.

Their revolution failed, not because of lack of ideas, but because of their lack of skills. Before going bush, they should have gone to "Giuseppe" or "Ngoc Tan," the vegetable growers who lived on the outskirts of their cities, and asked to be shown how to grow carrots, lettuce, and potatoes!

Our generation is a generation without masters. We are still under the impression, and like to think, that The Beatles didn't have to learn how to play music; that Jimi Hendrix picked up a guitar one morning, put a big joint in his mouth, and started to play like a god. Does this next, younger generation, understand that there cannot possibly be art without skill?

As the Zen masters advise, the brush moves by itself only after the movements have been internalized to such an extent that there is no distinction between the brush, the hand, and the mind moving it.

And Robert Pirsig in *Zen and the Art of Motorcycle Maintenance* had something to say not only about classic, or technical, beauty, that is the beauty of something which doesn't just look beautiful but performs beautifully, but also about the relationship between mind and hands. He **81** ▶ wrote: "Peace of mind produces right values, right values produce right thoughts. Right thoughts produce right action, and right actions produce work which will be a material reflection for others to see of the serenity at the center of it all."[4]

You may ask, how can you be at peace with yourself if you hate what you do? You can't. You have to love what you do to be at peace. It comes as no surprise then that successful people love what they do; they are passionate about it. They excel because there is no distinction in their minds between work and play, working and living.

Success, we can therefore say, is to do beautifully whatever it is that you love doing. Only when you are at peace with yourself can you master the skills to produce magnificent work. The urge to become what we ought to become is expressed by good work.

And successful people come from every social stratum, race, and sex. Some have been physically and psychologically abused; some couldn't see; some couldn't move and typed their books, letter by letter, with a stick held in their mouths. To be a genius in your own mind, however, is meaningless; you have to dance it, build it, grow it, communicate it. Share it with the world.

Is it possible to emerge from a stultifying life, refusing to be treated as an insignificant cog in the machine? Is it possible to reject values that enslave us and to surmount physical handicaps as well as psychological ones? Yes! But only when our mind, heart, and hands work together.

Tourists and lovers

"The place to improve the world is first in one's own heart and head and hands, and then work outward from there."

—— Robert Pirsig[5]

Let's go to work then, without cursing it. But let's only work at what we want to work at, at what we love doing, at what we were meant to do.

And let's teach our young that what counts is not only what they do, but also how they do it. That the quality of their mind, heart, and hands combined is what will make them successful. That it is much better to be a first-rate housewife than a second-rate physician. That their first duty is to develop themselves, to put in Schumacher's words, "their inner house in order" and to work from there outwardly.

Keith Bradby, the radical environmentalist who became a consultant to the Esperance farmers, used to say that there are two kinds of people: the lovers and the tourists. The lovers are those who love what they do, are committed to it, and are stayers, that is, they stick to it even in times of adversity. The tourists, on the contrary, like to move around: one day here, next day there, unattached and uncommitted.

There is no qualitative difference between the two. The tourist is looking for the ideal place with which to fall in love, has not found it as yet, but hopes, even longs to find it. The difference between the lovers and the tourists is one of timing. We all have the potential to be both, at different stages of our lives. Tourists can perform beautifully in casual jobs, gathering experiences and developing an interest that can become their own calling. The lovers have found what moves them. It may take a long time to realize it, but their course is set, the direction is clear, their life's task ahead of them.

Schumacher's quotation at the beginning of this chapter referred to setting up a sail "so that when the wind comes," we may catch it. To me, the wind is nothing but the energy generated by committed people with a dream to fulfill and the willingness to learn how to make it happen.

These are the lovers described above, and facilitators only work with lovers. Any attempt to work with "tourists" is futile, and unless this is understood, what follows won't make any sense.

9. TRAINING FACILITATORS

"The master said: The case is like that of someone raising a mound. If he stops working, the fact that it perhaps needed only one more basketful makes no difference; I stay where I am. Whereas even if he has not got beyond leveling the ground, but is still at work, the fact that he has only tilted one basketful of earth makes no difference, I go help him."

— Confucius[1]

FACILITATION IS BASED ON THE BELIEF THAT IT IS HUMAN TO DREAM and to desire. Faith in human nature is what makes it work. The absolute certainty that anywhere, at any time, there will be people who, having recognized what truly moves them, are committed to it and are thinking, planning, and working at making their dream become a material reality. This is true of all healthy people, of all those who are able, according to Maslow, to keep growing. From African villages to the steppes of Siberia, we can count on the human characteristic of always looking for something.

The skill of the facilitator is to become available to those who have the dream and to help them acquire the skills to transform it into meaningful and rewarding work. The skill of facilitation is therefore a communication skill with a twist. It isn't so much that facilitators have to communicate to their client; rather they have to be the kind of person one likes to talk to.

Facilitators are good listeners.

Einstein recalled in his biography the time when a student came to his study and spoke incessantly and, upon leaving, thanked Einstein, who had hardly uttered a word, for the great help and wonderful conversation!

Facilitators have the same quality. They get people to open up, to unburden, and to share their innermost thoughts. Carl Rogers wrote that in therapy, the facilitator simply removes the obstacles that stifle the client's growth. In other words, the clients have the ability to heal themselves if the obstacles in their way are removed.

Facilitators are passive.

To new Enterprise Facilitators, the idea that being passive is the beginning of communication often comes as a shock. Our action-crazy culture has little understanding of the wisdom of being passive. What did Lao-tzu mean when he wrote: "I take no action and the people are transformed of themselves?"[2] It sounds like a riddle, yet how many times do people ask for help, confide their problems and find the solution by simply talking about it? You have done nothing except to be there, attentive and caring. Facilitators do this all the time, but the ability to apply "active listening" doesn't come naturally to most of them. They have to learn to "shut up," and to give the clients the opportunity to talk about what is on their minds.

To be passive is the foundation of our work because by being passive, we are able to reverse the relationship of power and control between the clients and us.

If you arrive in a community and you start doing things, the community will immediately identify you as an expert, as somebody who is there to "develop" them; they will become spectators, watching you doing things to them, for them. You will probably be seen very rarely in public during working hours, your telephone will be busy, your office hidden away somewhere out of sight.

If you do that, you will never make it as a facilitator, because people will not come and confide in you. Firstly, you are too busy for them to come and waste your time, and secondly, because you are an expert — how can they possibly interest you in their petty ideas? Thirdly, you are difficult to meet, and finally, you are intimidating. Experts represent authority, and authority intimidates people.

Facilitators are visible.

There is a crossroad in Esperance, right in the middle of town. It has the Post Office on one corner, two banks diametrically opposed to each other, and a coffee bar on the fourth corner. The coffee bar has tables outside which command great views not only of the intersection, but also of the two main shopping areas in town.

There I would sit, drinking coffee and reading, every morning. People had to see me! Eventually the entire population of Esperance had to drive or walk past that spot. The message that I wanted to convey was: "Look, I'm doing nothing; if you want to talk to me, here I am."

85 ▶

It is true that I nearly got caffeine poisoning, but it is also true that after a few months I was introducing Esperance people to other Esperance people. Even in that small community, many locals had never met. Few people in the town were as visible and as accessible as I was, and I met a great number of people in a very short time.

And in a way, I was "naked," sitting under that umbrella at the crossroads café; I had no money to entice the locals, no programs, schemes, resources to bestow upon them. I had no ideas and no prejudices either. I didn't have a clue about what would happen next or who would approach me. But I was there, doing nothing, so they came to share a cappuccino and a dream with me.

The victim

An acquaintance of mine who is a chef calls his patrons his "victims." He tends to feed them to the point of indigestion and minor liver complaints! We jokingly refer to the first clients of new facilitators as "victims," too. In their enthusiasm to impress their clients and upon learning their secret ambitions, they tend to overwhelm them with a sudden flurry of activity. When the energy of new facilitators, who are determined to show their value and prove their worth, is finally released, if unchecked, it can leave their client running for cover dreading the day they first opened their mouths. Yes, they had a dream, but they didn't mean to mortgage their houses, employ seven people, and be bundled into an aircraft and dispatched to an international trade fair in the first month of activity!

The first client of new facilitators is the most important client they will ever have. The quality of the work done and the consequent results of their help will establish their reputation in the community and guarantee their future work. Enough time and care should therefore be dedicated to this first client, and even if three months are required to get his/her new business to open, then so be it. New facilitators don't advertise that they are in town. An ad in the local paper seldom produces real clients and often results in yet another cynical dismissal: "Oh, yes, another government scheme — another miracle cure!" The only way to be accepted and utilized by the community is to demonstrate one's worth. That first client offers that opportunity and should be treated accordingly.

Facilitators work in confidence.

Where do you find your first client? In all probability, a local agency or local incorporated body employ the facilitator. A small number of local people are thus available to them and they should be a good starting point.

The committee will introduce the facilitator to their friends and acquaintances. They can organize small social functions like tea parties or meet at the pub on Friday evening.

The facilitator is introduced as a person, not as a functionary. His/her role is explained as simply as possible, with one word always stressed: *confidential*. For example: "Mary here is available to anybody in town with an idea for a new business — anything you tell her will be held strictly confidential."

First clients are found by meeting people, socializing, and keeping your ears open. It isn't always easy, however; the first few weeks are the most difficult and can unnerve new facilitators. They seem to say, "Here I am, appointed, trained, paid to get things rolling, to bring new hope to the community, to make dreams come true, and nothing happens. Nobody comes around, stops me in the street, or ever joins me for a coffee. Could it be that there are no dreamers here? That among thousands of individuals, not even one has found or developed any interest in doing something new?"

This is definitely a high anxiety period and the temptation is very strong to start doing something. To do a bit of research on the economics of the region, to organize a training course for women in business, to do anything at all rather than waiting for something to happen.

Doing nothing, however, is the only thing facilitators should do.

"Go out for a walk, have a coffee," I would say over the phone to a new facilitator at his wits' end. After months, still no one had approached him. "I don't drink coffee!" he would shout back at me, "and even if I did, there are no coffee bars in this place!"

Then it finally happens, the first client is met, good work ensues, and things start to roll.

Micko O'Byrne, the facilitator who didn't drink coffee, was asked to help in bottling water — rainwater, to be more exact. The publicity from the launch of that business was such that he went, in 12 months, from obscurity to being presented with an industry award by the local city council. He had helped 40 businesses in that period but still reeled at the thought of his initial three months of maddening inactivity.

In the initial period in a new community, facilitators have to act as swans, that is, deport themselves in a dignified, calm manner while paddling water furiously under the surface as they are actively looking for their first client and the chance to demonstrate that even in that community there are good people with good ideas and that, yes, with a bit of help you can transform their dreams into reality.

Action at last

> "Whatever you can do or dream you can begin it. Boldness has genius, magic and power in it. Begin it now."
>
> — Goethe

Facilitators love action; the fact that they seem so passive, act "cool" and never initiate any projects is because they know that unless there is a committed individual driving the project, no matter how good the idea is, it will not succeed.

They are as passive as a loaded spring ... they wait.

When their first real, committed, self-motivated client asks for help, they can finally spring into action and put all their energy behind the project. And the first project is always special, never to be forgotten, rather like a first love. For one thing, the facilitator has all the time in the world to work at it. Remember that nobody had asked for help and that there had been nothing to do. So now time and pent-up energy are finally put to good use with feelings of trepidation and release.

Finally at work

The client in front of you could be wanting to do anything, from exporting frozen paratemia[3] (it happened to me and I didn't know what the client was talking about!) to setting up a mobile repair service for farmers.

Where do you start? Do you assess the person or the idea?

The facilitator has to start with the person and the motivation behind the idea. Ideas, you will soon learn in this job, are cheap. We all have them; we all generate ideas, even good ones that go nowhere. Passionate individuals prepared to mortgage their houses and to put everything on the line to make their ideas work are rare, and without them, nothing happens. So, no matter what the idea is like, initially the facilitator should concentrate on the proponent and listen attentively to find out whether there is serious commitment there.

In training facilitators, we suggest that they listen to their clients with their entire being, meaning that they don't only use their rational mind but also their instincts, or their power of observation, in assessing the proponent's motivation. How committed are their clients? How long have they been trying to start this business? How angry are they? How frustrated? Why do they want to do this? What is their motivation? Money? Fulfillment? Do they really love it?

If the facilitator listens carefully, he/she begins to get "vibes" — that is, are the clients confident, relaxed, nervous, mistrusting? Communication can be difficult. The clients can be defensive or withdrawn. Maybe the facilitator gets the feeling that the clients are not telling everything, that some of the truth is missing. It is imperative to confront those feelings and to reconcile what has been said with what is felt about the client.

The clients can be saying how confident they are, when your impression instead is one of insecurity and ego-tripping. Could it be that they are is trying to impress you? Do they act this way when confronted with "authority"? Could they be intimidated by you? Is their showing-off a defense? Are they not trusting you and withholding information on purpose? Could it be that they are simply checking you out before telling you the real story?

Obviously the quality of the person will determine the quality of the business and its chances of success. Before a facilitator risks everything to help their first clients, shouldn't he/she understand them as much as possible?

Facilitators spend time and effort establishing true communication with clients. A very good reason to create a trusting relationship with the client is that inevitably the question of money will come up. This is always a delicate matter.

People play games with each other, we assume roles with people we don't know, and can mask our true feelings. Some of the games people play when confronted with what they perceive as the powerful are the following:

- I am the client (the baby); you are the expert (the parent)

- I am a frustrated genius (misunderstood and broke); you are the government who has to help me (fat cat)

- I am cute and naive (virgin lost in the woods); you are strong and powerful (and will take care of me)

- I am an inventor (therefore unable to do more than one thing at a time); you are a manager (take a share of my business and we will become rich together).[4]

Facilitators don't play power games.

To avoid such interpersonal games, there is only one thing the facilitator can do: avoid being mistaken or identified as a power figure.

It is also in this respect that being passive is so strongly advocated and will pay dividends. People will tend to treat facilitators differently from other "public servants" only if facilitators behave differently. If they do not hide in their office, behind desks and secretaries. If they do not wear expensive "power" suits, ties, shoulder pads, and other dress symbols. If they are seen in public, mixing with "normal" people and behaving like them.

Facilitators should realize that if good communication is not achieved, it is probably their fault. The fact that someone made an effort to seek out and initiate a meeting should be a good indication that this person needs something. It is up to the facilitator to make their clients relax and feel they are talking to people who, apart from their technical skills, are decent, caring human beings. Are the clients secretive? Tell them that everything they say will be kept confidential. Are they nervous? Check yourself and your surroundings. Are you sitting opposite or side by side with the client?

Are you in public or in private? Should you offer to go and see their workshops and become a guest in their territory? Nothing makes people feel more at ease than inviting you into their kitchen and offering you a cup of tea or coffee .... Unless their house is a mess and they have rejected your offer to visit them!

Interpersonal skills are skills that are learnt from childhood and are constantly refined. Unfortunately one can only hope that people appointed to be facilitators already possess these, because they cannot be taught easily, and certainly not within the confines of this book.

Good facilitators are nonthreatening, unassuming, friendly listeners who make people want to talk to them. They are the ultimate people's people. They manage to get a feeling for the person in front of them until one day they will be certain that they have finally found a "lover:" someone who is prepared to fully engage in a new venture.

The first project

You have found it. The first client is in front of you, and you are satisfied that this person wants to commit fully to a project. He or she is self-motivated, determined, and resolute. There could be some frustration, even anger present at not having already achieved what he or she had hoped for but there will also definitely be energy and eagerness.

Now is the time to look at the idea.

An example: The client is a married farmer tired of the usual farm practices, and she is determined to put 10 out of the family's 2,000-acre farm under intensive agriculture. She tells you that she wants to grow lavender. "Why lavender?" you ask. And she tells you that she read an article on lavender farming in a magazine and she thought it was a good idea.

You ask her whether she wants to make an income from it or whether she loves lavender. She replies that it really isn't important what she grows, she just wants to grow something different which is her own crop and which can provide her with an alternative source of income.

"Shouldn't we find out what kind of soil you have on your property and draw up a list of possible crops for you to grow?" you say. In other words, you explore her true motivation before offering advice on lavender farming, which in this case was not the exclusive interest of the client.

But what happens if the client wants to grow lavender, and only lavender? Her motivation is to have acres of mauve flowers surrounding her farmhouse, no matter whether the commercial price for lavender is reasonable or not. What do you do?

You help her make a success out of it, and if the price of lavender is low, you explore secondary products which could be marketed as part of a lavender farm, for example having tourist chalets among the fields, producing her own beauty products from lavender, selling dried herbs for aromatherapy, inventing a new product altogether.

The above example should indicate that facilitators don't provide data on products; rather, they give critical advice. They don't take a client's first request as a completely matured and well-structured proposal. They are not passive anymore.

This is the time to analyze the idea, and not remember, to draw out the person. The client is there, alert, open and trusting you. The facilitator now has to help assess the potential of the idea within the parameters that the client has set.

The chief parameter is the finances and resources available to the client. For instance, ten acres of irrigation would be manageable, but 2,000 would be out of the question. The project has, therefore, to be scaled to ten acres, and every projection will have to be based on that.

What can the client invest into the project? Does the client have access to finance? This is the time when the dream momentarily touches ground. Money is always seen as a problem. "If only I had one thousand dollars, one million, ten million," they say.

No matter how much or how little your clients have, they will always tell you that they are short of money. Why? Because otherwise they would not be dreamers; they would be living within their means, accepting their lot and being content with what they have.

By definition, our clients want something that they don't have, and money is often what they believe they lack but 90% of the time they are, *wrong*.

The management trinity

> "Entrepreneurship in society — and it is badly needed — requires above all application of the basic concepts, the basic techniques of management to new problems and new opportunities."
>
> — P. Drucker[5]

Bad management kills companies, not lack of finance. No matter how much money you infuse into a badly managed business, the chances of it succeeding are slim, whereas if you infuse good management into a financially troubled company, you can expect it to turn around. The literature available on this subject is vast and conclusive.

This is to say that people, not money, run businesses.

Therefore, a grasp of the fundamentals of management is required before we engage in successful facilitation. No matter how big or small a business is, three areas of activities need to be taken care of:

- the technical skills necessary to produce the goods or services one wishes to sell (whether they be shoes or package tours);
- the ability to market one's goods or services;
- the ability to financially manage one's affairs.

These three areas I call the "Management Trinity." If any one of the above is missing, the business is not a business, it shouldn't be called one, and it will never succeed.

It comes as no surprise, then, that in assessing the potential success of the client's idea, the facilitator should ascertain which of the three aspects of the business the client can take care of and, more importantly, which areas would be left wanting.

It must be said at this point that it is extremely difficult to find a person who is capable of competently carrying out all three functions. Personally, I have never met anyone who could produce the product, market it, and manage the finances of the business. Plenty of people try to do it, many do it badly, but nobody I have ever met has been equally passionate and proficient in all three areas.

Often a client will be talented in producing and selling the product, or in producing and organizing the financial bookkeeping. What is very rare is to find someone who is equally passionate about marketing and bookkeeping.

Could it be that we only excel at doing what we love? Could it be that marketing and financial management require different personalities? Extroverts and introverts? Even discounting psychology, we know that one thing is very clear: successful businesses are always a team effort. Whether it is a husband-and-wife team or a corporate structure, successful businesses are built around people's skills. That's why personnel recruiting firms do so well: a great deal of effort is spent finding the right person for the job. A good team can succeed in nearly everything.

Find the people, form the team

> "You won't go anywhere without good people. Hear me now. Don't forget this. They don't have to be geniuses. It doesn't hurt to have some. But, by and large, you can get by with good, solid 120 IQ people if they are motivated, dedicated, honest, generous people who can work together."
>
> — John Masters[6]

At the beginning there is one person with an idea. Before you can have a business, one has to become three. It is a bit theological but the symbolism hopefully will help to recall this simple truth.

It could be that two people can cover three functions, but still all three functions have to be adequately covered. An example is Mauri, who could produce smoked fish very well; he was pretty good at selling his product too, but lacked financial skill. The fishermen were good at producing sashimi-quality tuna, pretty good with finances (at least two of them were) but needed help with marketing their product.

The role the facilitator plays is, to first of all, put a mirror in front of the client and to say "Look, you are alone, how can you perform these three functions?"

Facilitators help to find the missing team members.

Here our wit, cunning, experience, talent, or whatever you want to call it comes into play. How do you co-opt people into nonexistent businesses that are often underresourced and undercapitalized?

You have to package your client's dream and sell it. You have to become an advocate for lavender farms, smoked fish, and so on. You have to extol the virtues of such enterprises and to convince one or two other people to become involved in the project in question. In a sense you momentarily fulfill the marketing role of the "would-be" company with the added psychological advantage that you are more credible since you have no financial involvement in it.

To fill the Trinity is simple if the client can employ or remunerate people. Unfortunately, not many can do so in the early stages of the business. We therefore have to use a different strategy. Here are some which I have used and can recommend:

- Beg

Ask a friendly accountant or marketing person to help for free, at least for the first few months — incredibly, it often works!

- Promise something you don't have

Offer a "success fee," which means that you promise to reward by sharing future profits.

- Give shares in your worthless company

Form a company and allocate shares to those who come on board. Remember to keep enough shares to allocate to future equity investors, the people who will put hard cash into the venture.

- Find volunteer help

Convince somebody to volunteer to help you! This is similar to begging but is usually reserved for people with whom you have a bit of influence, namely your spouse, best friend, parents, etc.

There are terrific examples of partnerships that have developed around what was once a very private dream. Passionate people are often "infectious;" they tend to attract others. A passionate client and a passionate facilitator shouldn't have too much difficulty in building a working team.

It is only when you have a working team that you as a facilitator are officially in business. If this is your first project, then you have the advantage of having time to nurture it. Time should be utilized helping the team to research information and resources needed to take the project from concept to reality. The facilitator plays a significant role all the way down the line right to the official opening of this first new business in town.

Nothing succeeds like success, and a satisfied and happy first client will become the facilitator's greatest ally in convincing the community that this innovative way of doing things is worth supporting.

The helper helped

> "Without the help of Ernesto Sirolli I couldn't possibly have
> made it."
> — Mauri Green, quoted in *The Esperance Express* (1985.)

The facilitator will ask the client for help. "You have to help me," one says to an often-surprised client. "Me, help you?" is often the answer. "How?"

You have to explain that very few people in the community understand what you do for the client. That even after you tell them what you do, it is not believed, and that your future as a facilitator depends on people using you. You need your clients to help promote your work, to do for you a bit of the advocacy that you did for them.

Since the opening of a new business makes good copy, it shouldn't be difficult to have the local newspaper send someone out to take a picture and write a story. Ask the client to promote the business first and to help you second. Try to be there in the story for the community to read about. Remember that it is only at the point when one member of a community is prepared to stand up for you that you start to have a chance of being accepted. Until then you have only been watched. People with ideas, energy, motivation, and even money have simply been looking at you and waiting to see if you can perform or not.

Now they will start coming round. Your name and face have been seen in the local paper, associated with a success story. All of a sudden you will notice a change around you — people smile at you in the street, they acknowledge your existence and even come and sit with you at the crossroads café.

Months of high anxiety have gone by. First doing nothing and keeping your cool, then doing a great deal with your first client. Now you start to get the rewards. People start to seek you out to talk about their dreams. You are becoming busy, very busy; there is no time anymore to cultivate your clients, to mother them — you have to shift gear and change strategy.

Network

> "I have to keep networking everywhere, looking for good partners."
> — Steve Wayne[7]

Brian, the first facilitator I trained, had 45 clients after only two months. He was, in his own words, going mad! He was carrying out marketing research and feasibility studies and writing business plans — a huge amount of work. He had been so adamant that "nobody" would use his services during our initial twenty-minute training session that he had not even reached the point of asking me, "But what if they come? What should I do then?"

After two months, he asked me to return to Esperance to see him. He admitted he had been wrong and then asked me how one could possibly work with so many clients without going insane? "They ring me at home in the evenings," he complained, "they come around on weekends."

Following in my footsteps, he had a fast, instead of a typical slow start, which required a stage-two strategy. Remember that stage one is keeping your cool, finding your "victim", and publicizing your role.

Stage two is getting organized to deal with many clients by finding out who in the community can fulfill some of the roles to make that particular project happen. Getting to know capable people, creating an informal network of professionals, co-opting like-minded locals to volunteer their services — these are the next tasks to which the facilitator must attend.

In keeping with the principle of the "Trinity," each project has to be strengthened by you finding suitable and interested team members. Look among your local financial and business managers, such as accountants, bankers, and retired business people. They should be approached and their support enlisted. Knowing how to find out who is capable and willing to help becomes vital at this stage.

You have to realize that your limited time is now better utilized in identifying people who can join your client in an ongoing commercial relationship than in trying to do it all yourself. Who in the network can take on the work that will see the business take off? How do you find people interested in marketing honey? Wildflowers? Or electronic components?

One has to be out there in the marketplace, living, breathing facilitation. Information is gathered by talking to people, by inquiring, and even by hassling. It is not possible in this profession to have a database ready to work from. How can one prepare the answers if one doesn't know the questions? Facilitators deal with such a variety of topics that most of the work is information gathering on a case-by-case basis. Databases have the disadvantage of aging quickly, and commercial information needs to be current. Your client needs today's price of lavender oil, not last year's. You have to source information and to find personnel and physical **97** resources on demand and quickly.

Yes, it is possible to have a small number of professionals at hand, especially in business management areas, but most of our work is still spent trying to find out who locally, statewide, nationwide can help a specific client to commercialize a unique product.

Good facilitators are not shy, they ring and ask.

Somebody wrote that it is possible to put two people in touch, even if they are from different continents and speak different languages, via a maximum of five intermediary contacts. Apparently, it was attempted a number of times and always worked. The trick was to start with someone who had a contact in the country where the person to be reached lived; then someone the region, the town, etc. would be contacted until one reached someone who knew the person in question.

Facilitators play this game all the time, only they do it "blindfolded" in the sense that they often don't know whether there is a person at the other end to help fill their client's need. Facilitators become a repository of contacts and information. They collect business cards, newspaper articles, trivia, and gossip. Above all, they don't know — and should not be ashamed of saying so: "I don't know, mate. I have never exported donkey skin jelly to China. I didn't even know that the Chinese eat the stuff but leave it with me and I will find out how we can do it."

One comforting thing for anyone who wants to do this job is that people only dream the dreamable and imagine the imaginable. In other words, no matter how far-fetched an idea seems, it will still be possible to analyze it by rational, commercial, and scientific thinking.

The great majority of ideas people have are of an imitative nature, and you seldom get completely stuck for words. However, I have to admit that years ago I was asked to help a gentleman who wanted to reactivate underwater dormant volcanoes with dynamite. He wanted to do this to provide a tourist attraction, and I can say that he blew me away. This was the one time I had a sinking feeling about my profession!

A final word of caution, notwithstanding my "volcano man." Don't dismiss crazy ideas. It is so rare to find something truly original that to dismiss it out of hand is a terrible waste. You have to reach your clients to assess their chances of their business succeeding. Try to listen with an open mind to everything and everybody. In our job we cannot afford to be cynical or to prejudge people. We have to take everybody at face value and to accept that we will be taken for a ride now and then. It is not for us to say to the clients that their ideas are stupid and not commercially viable. There is a way to help them to find this out for themselves without making them feel bad about it.

The "back of the envelope" business plan

> "Suppose a project consists of 10 key steps; further imagine that the odds of making it through any one step are 70%. What are the odds of surviving all 10 steps? The correct probability is .7x.7x.7x.7x-.7x.7x.7x.7x.7x.7 or 3%."
>
> — Tom Peters[8]

Grab a piece of paper — an old envelope will do, a serviette if you're sitting at a café, or a beer coaster — and ask your client the following:

- How much money do you need to make every week out of this new business to survive?

- How many hamburgers/alarm-systems/packs of donkey skin jelly do you need to sell to make that much after expenses? At what price do you need to sell them? If they don't know, ask them to take a guess.

- How many kilos of meat? At what cost? How much rent? How much goodwill do they have to pay for the hamburger business?

- Have they thought about insurance, utilities, and similar costs?

Write down, there and then, those approximate figures, even guesses, for the client to see. It could become immediately evident that it would take selling 10,000 hamburgers a week, every week of the year, to make a living. Is it achievable?

You have to get your clients to flesh out their ideas by understanding that the fundamentals have to add up. Show them, no matter how roughly, what is meant by the "bottom line," what it will take to simply survive in the business for a time.

The last line of your scribbles is the one that shows a profit or a loss. It is not for you to discourage or encourage a client to embark on a new venture. It is for you to help to assess at this very early stage whether or not conditions exist to even consider such a venture. This exercise should be, for your clients, a taste of things to come. They should understand that for their dream to become a viable and a rewarding activity, they will have to learn how to ask appropriate questions and to come up with answers that are as accurate as possible.

Only two things can happen after this very first look at the figures: the client is convinced either to carry on with the idea or to abandon it. If the first look at the figures is not positive, and this happens a great percentage of the time, you have probably managed to save the client quite a lot of money that may have otherwise been wasted in trying to start up an business that isn't viable.

If the idea after this very early and superficial examination stacks up, and the client is determined to proceed, then make a time to meet again to talk serious business.

The true business plan

You have in front of you a self-motivated, energetic client who has sought your assistance and who has met you on several occasions. Together, you have broadly assessed the viability of the would-be business and have discussed, and agreed upon, the need to eventually co-opt people to help (the Trinity).

It is now time to find out how serious, and smart, the client is and there is no better way of knowing that than to present him/her with a blank model business plan. Facilitators have such model plans ready. They can be as long as 60 pages, and oblige clients to ask and answer a host of pertinent questions about their future business.

Ask your client to look at the business plan and to start thinking about which parts of it he/she would feel excited to complete. Is it the description of the product, the marketing strategy, or the financial projections that the client feel competent about and ready to put into words?

As mentioned in the chapter concerning the Management Trinity, we have never met a single human being who loves the three areas equally. Your client will very quickly identify areas of competence, and you will then be able to point at areas of incompetence and suggest that a team be assembled to produce the best business plan they are capable of writing. Such a document should be good enough to guide management during the early stages of the business and to assist in securing funding. The emphasis on teamwork, at this early but critical time in the development of the enterprise, distinguishes our work from what is suggested by entrepreneurial educators who put great emphasis on business plan preparation as necessary learning for would-be entrepreneurs.

We agree on the need for the individual entrepreneur to understand the different management responsibilities required to run a successful business, but we strongly caution the entrepreneur against attempting to become what they are not. If they hate financial management, our experience tells us that they will be bad financial managers, no matter how many training manuals they read.

The problems for self-styled entrepreneurs, who have started their business after successfully completing a course on business plan writing will appear when the first real crisis hits the new business. Under stress, they will revert to character and will start doing what they do the best.

If they are marketing personalities, they will be marketing like crazy and will go broke because their costing is wrong or they cannot produce enough to fill orders. If they are product people, they will manufacture without orders and create new products that nobody wants, and if they are financial management people, they will sit in front of their computer screens cutting all the company's costs and losing both product and marketing people!

Enterprise Facilitators will impress upon their clients that the complete entrepreneur doesn't exist and that the smart entrepreneur is the one who learns the secret of business success, that is, to have passionate people doing what they love best in the different areas of management.

When such a team prepares the business plan, the document that they produce is "bankable," that is, it can attract finances from institutional or private lenders.

One of the questions that is often asked of facilitators is how an individual with no or few resources can attract a team. Facilitators and their community boards are there exactly to break the isolation of the clients and to use community networks to find temporary or long-term team members. As in the story of the Esperance fishermen or Rollie in South Dakota, the role of the Enterprise Facilitator is to explain the need for the team to the client and actively to assist in its formation.

No large- or medium-size company could operate without the separation of management roles we have described. The fact that small business and entrepreneurial training still insist on one individual doing it all puzzles me. Could the false belief in a team of one be the cause for the massive failure rate of small businesses in the first five years of activity? How come small business failures do not diminish even though small business courses and entrepreneurial education increase?

101 ▶

No successful entrepreneur has ever succeeded alone; the biographies of such people are a public record of the struggles, efforts, and compromises that they had to endure to find and keep the partners and associates who made their vision reality.

There are hundreds of books, manuals, and computer programs dealing with drawing up business plans. There is a cult about them, and it is very easy, in every country, to find models to use as guides. But if the technique is pretty straightforward, what is less understood is that people, not theories, run companies and that a perfect business plan is totally useless if the people who have to implement it are incapable of doing so.

From pie in the sky to — real cake

The genesis of a business can be long and arduous. Murphy's Law also applies, and whatever can go wrong often does!

It isn't the rich or the healthy who survive, and even the strong can be broken. The entrepreneur who can survive is, in my experience, the one who is not alone on the journey. A Bible saying reiterates this: "A friend supported by a friend is like an impregnable fortress."

I see the development of a business as a process of accumulating wills and talents, and the role of the facilitator is one of providing a first, albeit temporary, traveling companionship to the client. If initially the client's dream looks like a "pie in the sky," with dedication it could end up looking like an appetizing cake. Like a cake, it is made of successive layers representing more and more talents, information, motivation, and resources.

The very thin pancake you may have glimpsed during the first interview starts to look more substantial as the client comes back a second and then third time. A partner joins in, a friend volunteers help, and all of a sudden the shadow of a cake appears. A full business plan is prepared, a first investor joins in, manufacturing contracts are entered into, distributorship agreements are signed, more people are putting their time and energy behind the project. Now we have a cake, and we may even be able to put some icing on it by floating the company and having more people put more funds in.

All the way through we have seen people joining forces, pooling resources and know-how. More importantly, we have seen diverse skills at work complementing each other to fulfill the requirements of business.

Recently, I was asked by a development agency what the criteria were that they should use in screening would-be entrepreneurs who were asking for government funding. They receive an average of 500 applications per year and can fund only 50 of these. The applications include business plans and personal interviews, but the agency found it difficult to make a selection.

My advice was, firstly, to give up the idea that they could pick "winners" — nobody can do that. Secondly, I suggested that if they really wanted to maximize their chances of finding prospective new entrepreneurs, they should look at who, among the applicants, was a team builder. The person who is most capable of enlisting the support of others is the most likely to succeed.

10. A Word of Caution

IF PEOPLE DON'T WANT TO BE HELPED, LEAVE THEM ALONE.

Facilitators are not welfare workers and should only work with "lovers." This seems straightforward but in practice, it is difficult to let go of an excellent business idea which has already withstood the test of an accurate business plan, marketing research, and even guaranteed finance.

An example from Esperance: a couple had developed and researched the feasibility of a tourist attraction to be located in a disused building on the town's main street. The local council loved the idea and gave its approval, the bank was ready to lend to the proponents, and it looked more than promising. Brian could just about see the local newspaper headlines about more jobs created with the help of the facilitator.

The morning his clients were supposed to sign the finance documents, they went to see Brian to tell him that they were too afraid to put so much money on the line and didn't want to go on with the project anymore.

I wasn't there to see Brian's face, but being a good facilitator, he must have swallowed hard, and then sent them on their way with a smile. No hard feelings — it was their project, their risk, not Brian's, and if they ever changed their minds and came back to it, he would help them again with the same respect and commitment.

Remember that the client's idea is confidential, so no matter how good it would be for your community, the facilitator cannot divulge or suggest it to anyone else. The short-term gain from opening a new business in town using a client's idea would destroy the integrity of the "office" of the facilitator, and people would be reluctant to part with their ideas if confidentiality wasn't assured.

The facilitator's commitment to the project is proportionate to the client's own commitment. If a client drops the project, so does the facilitator. No questions asked, no guilt implied. Facilitators do not ring clients, they ring them back. If clients disappear, leave them alone. It could very well be that they have changed their minds or have financial difficulties, family problems, or simply lost interest.

The best thing to do is to wait for them to reappear, and if they never do, keep a friendly and positive attitude. Remember that it is their lives we deal with. Hands off. then, both physically and psychologically.

Facilitators don't coerce, convince, manipulate, or motivate clients.

We don't try to make things happen no matter the cost. We don't hold the economic development of the town in higher esteem than our individual client. Nothing, not headlines, possible jobs, or money to be made will make us jettison our clients' trust. Motivational theory doesn't work — anyone who has tried to motivate their own children will agree with this.

And thank God for it. Because if it did work, we would be in the unenviable position of presiding over the disrupted lives of those we have motivated. To me, there is not a more pathetic sight than a person who has been manipulated into a career or enterprise that has nothing to do with his/her inclinations and natural talents.

Fortunately, only very few people endure the agony for long, and we can look to literature and Hollywood movies to provide ample examples (some of them very funny) of what happens when people rebel against psychological repression. Having found the courage, they walk into the boss's/lion's den and ... tell them what to do with their jobs!

A more subtle and pernicious form of mind control can happen without the facilitator noticing it. It is called transference, and it is a professional hazard for all those involved in person-to-person counseling. Basically people — men/women/young/old — simply fall in love with you and do everything you say, not because it may help to realize what they really want, but to please you. They need your recognition and endorsement and can become fixated in their efforts to please you.

Doctors and psychiatrists are taught about it and know how to deal with transference. Facilitators should also know about it and be prepared. My advice in this situation is to be a little bit rude to clients who are clingy. We should reiterate that it is their project, their lives, their work, their money — that we don't care for one project more than for another, that we help everybody.

Answer

No! We are not going to spending more time with them than other clients.

No! We are not going to check on their progress every day.

No! We are not going to pat them on the back or patronize them.

And

No! We are not going to give them our holiday telephone number!

Does this remind you of stories of clients in therapy who do fine until their psychiatrist goes on holiday and then they collapse into a neurotic heap? They are "in love" with their analysts and act to please them. When their doctor goes on holidays, they see it as abandonment and even betrayal and react by throwing tantrums.

Avoid at all cost creating any dependency. "Abandon" your clients from that very first meeting, get them to understand that for you, they are just another client in a busy working day. Time for friendship will come, some of your clients will become good friends, but only when you deal with mature, assertive and adult personalities.

Tê

"Tê is what happens 'By the grace of God' as distinct from human striving .... It is also the unusual and thus remarkable naturalness of the sage, his unselfconscious and uncontrived skill in handling social and practical affairs, which John Lilly calls 'coincidence control.'"

— Alan Watts[1]

In closing this central section on facilitation, I cannot avoid mentioning that no matter how accurately you follow these suggestions, you will never make a good facilitator unless you can also "control coincidences." Serendipity, coincidence control, or Tê asserts that things only happen to those who do not try to make them happen. In other words, the more you force yourself, the more you exert yourself, the more you "will" life to deliver the results, the more the results you want will elude you.

Facilitators who succeed have no expectations, no plans of action, no targets, and no performance criteria to fulfill. They treat gently, they force nothing, they hardly leave a footprint on the sand. Things happen as if by magic — but it isn't magic. Things happen because they have faith in people, because they are positive about their work and serene in the manner they carry it out. They are not personally involved in clients or in outcomes.

Some don't believe in "coincidence control" and call it luck or "good timing." Good facilitators are then the lucky ones or, if you wish, lucky facilitators are the good ones.

Attitude is what makes the difference. No matter how visible, accessible, trustworthy you are, if you feel, deep down, that people are worthless, that no one with a worthwhile idea will ever come to you; if you feel that you are a leader of people, a "doer," and a manager; if you are insecure about your own worth, concerned about your future, and unhappy about your personal life, then you may sit at the crossroads café forever and nobody will ever join you.

Facilitators are successful people who love to see others succeed.

If, in your heart, you have never experienced success, don't try to make others successful. It would be like attempting to rescue someone from drowning without being able to swim.

Admonition Schumacher's to put "your inner house in order" is particularly relevant for those who embark on helping others. Once you are at peace, suspend judgement and belief and almost without you noticing, you will be talking to your first client.

PART THREE

THE FUTURE

11. Facilitation and Economic Development

"The market is frightening, even terrifying. It's not pretty. It's surely irrational, yet over the long haul, the unfettered market works for the most rational of reasons; it produces more experiments, more tries, more wins, more losses, more information processes (market signals) faster than any alternative."

— Tom Peters[1]

ENTERPRISE FACILITATION WORKS BECAUSE IT ENCOURAGES MORE people to seriously think about entering the business arena.

We know that in a year, in a community of 10,000 people, between 150 and 200 clients will see the local facilitator. Out of these, between 25 and 35 will open a new business or expand an existing one. Between 25 and 60 new jobs will be created with a combined annual turnover of between $5 and $10 million.

"Business success is," according to Peters, "the occasional (and usually accidental) by-product of the far more numerous failures."[2] This is why facilitators will always have one over planners and development corporation boards. We get involved with hundreds of projects, whereas they paint themselves into a corner trying to pick "winners" and restricting therefore the numbers of those at the starting blocks.

Nobody can pick winners; there is only safety in numbers. Nobody can predict the shape of tomorrow's market either, nor where the future profit areas will be. Economies which rely heavily on few starters and products are immensely more vulnerable than the ones which are diversified.

There are about ten million companies in Japan employing fewer than 30 workers each. Of these, nearly seven million are manufacturing companies. How many more Japanese are, at this very moment, thinking about going into private enterprise?

The nation with the broader "catchment" area will be the leader of tomorrow, not because it produces geniuses or particularly hard workers, but because it tries more.

Being there, getting involved in the market place, is the only way to learn how to succeed. Oscar Wilde wrote: "If you want to succeed in life, do something — the others are doing nothing!" Failure should be taken for what it really is: a lesson on the way to success — and the drama is taken out of it.

Some critics of Enterprise Facilitation are concerned with the rate of small business failures and imply that it is worthless to assist people to start a small business when its chances of succeeding are statistically slim. How silly! What is the alternative — only starting big businesses?

The idiocy of such criticism is obvious when one looks at the figures for both jobs and turnover generated by small businesses everywhere in the world. Individual entrepreneurs are the powerhouse of the economy — full stop.

It is obvious that economic prosperity depends on the quality of the people at the starting blocks, not on the size of the swimming pool nor on the quality of the water in it.

The wealth of nations

> "We can't improve the quality of our prisons until we get a better class of inmates!"
>
> — Ex-governor of Georgia

Like the Georgian governor who couldn't improve his prisons until he got a better class of inmates, so too a country won't get a better economic performance until it gets better and more people involved in creating wealth.

The thesis put forward in this book, that economic development has to do with people more than with the natural advantages of a country, requires a clarification. There is much more to the wealth of a nation than the growth of its GNP. The debate on how to achieve prosperity should therefore never be restricted to economics alone, but take into consideration the other qualities that inspire our society. No matter how rich Russia is in terms of natural resources, no matter how much arable land Argentina has, no matter how much fossil fuel Iraq produces, in the final analysis what makes a society prosper or not is the collective quality of its citizens.

These abilities and collective qualities are expressed not only in the fulfillment of material needs and the mastery of economic matters. They have to be expressed by equitable laws that create the foundations for peaceful social interactions, tolerance, freedom; for the collective care for the young, the aged, and the infirm; the respect for the environment and the inalienable personal rights to growth, self-fulfillment, and happiness.

111▶

The shift advocated by governments away from resource-driven economies to value-added ones cannot take place without recognizing that our greatest assets are not the ones that lie underground. Our greatest assets must be our energy, imagination, and skill — our commitment to good work and to the pursuit of excellence and the courage to fulfill our ambitions. Every single person is important in the creation of a better, wealthier, smarter society. Whether employed or not, engaged in export or service industries, in the arts, sports, or tourism, the *quality*, both personal and professional, of every single person is what will make a country prosperous.

The shift advocated here has at its core the development of infrastructures that will make it possible for everyone to "have a go." This book advocates the development of a supportive society: not one of handouts and protectionism, but one that recognizes the intrinsic value of individual, social, and commercial enterprises and that facilitates the transformation of good ideas into rewarding work.

The role of government of supporting such a change needs to be both proactive (top-down) and responsive (bottom-up). It will have to encourage a change in attitudes towards work and success and to provide infrastructures to facilitate this development. It will also need to be responsive to requests for assistance and to provide entrepreneurs with the information, advice, and resources appropriate to individual needs.

What will not work

"Planning as the term is commonly understood is actually incompatible with an entrepreneurial society...indeed the opportunities for innovation are found, on the whole, only way down and close to events. They are not to be found in the massive aggregates with which the planner deals of necessity, but in the deviations therefrom — in the unexpected, in the incongruity, in the difference between "the glass is half full" and "the glass is half empty," in the weak link in a process. "By the time the deviation becomes 'statistically significant' and thereby visible to the planner, it is too late. Innovative opportunities do not come with the tempest but with the rustling of the breeze."

— P. Drucker[3]

112 I had arrived in Esperance on the same weekend that 80 local people had shut themselves into a room on a property outside town to conduct a three-day brainstorming session. This initiative was the first step towards a one-year planning exercise in which seven subcommittees had to come up with specific recommendations in fields such as agriculture, fisheries, transport, tourism, etc. While the good citizens of Esperance were busy imagining the future of their town, I walked the streets asking that very stupid question which led me to meet my first client: "Do you know anybody who wants to do anything?"

When the strategic plan for Esperance finally saw the light, one year and many thousands of dollars later, it didn't contain any of the industries that we had created during that year. The planners, as usual, could not foresee what local people would come up with.

One of the recommendations of the fisheries committee was to write to the British fishing fleet operators to invite them to fish out of Esperance during the off-season. The problem, however, was that because of their size, the British vessels would not be able to use the newly built multimillion dollar Fishermen's Harbor. The committee therefore recommended that letters be written to the Minister for Marine and Harbors to ask that funds be provided to deepen the harbor so they could then write to England!

When the same subcommittee was asked whether they could help raise $1,000 towards the tuna fishermen's research, they refused on the grounds that the local fishermen were not to be trusted, that they "would never make it." I was so incensed that when finally the strategic plan (in two volumes) was released, I made it known that I believed the next time they produced such a document, they should at least print it on soft paper — so people could make some use of it.

It was cruel, I know, and I made some enemies, but I could not accept that the preparation of a "wish list" should take priority over real blood and sweat. That a bunch of local "aristocrats," that is, people with money or time or influence, should spend thousands of dollars of public money publishing their personal thoughts as if such thoughts embodied some form of superior wisdom, and should take priority over "real" enterprise. It seemed very arrogant to me and typical of top-down decision-making in general.

There is a role for planning — but not in generating innovation. Innovation starts between the ears of people, and planners can't see in there. **113** Facilitators can't either; that is why they spend such a long time trying to get people to tell them what it is that they are thinking.

The map is not the territory

"Map making is not the whole of philosophy just as a map or guidebook is not the whole of geography."[4] This warning found in one of Schumacher's books should be carved on the desk of every planner around the world.

In numerous discussions with friends and colleagues who are convinced of the values of planning, I have taken the position that it's time that this particular sacred cow was sent to the abattoirs. In my view, planning is a millstone around the necks of people who are subjected to it.

Planning is only as good as the planners themselves. From urban to economic planning, the documented history of disasters is comprehensive. Less well-documented and to my knowledge hardly noticed at all are the successes and achievements which come about spontaneously through inspiration, intuition, luck, and even by mistake.

Was the beauty of Venice planned? Or was the unlikely site for that city the result of coastal populations escaping the invading Huns? The juxtaposition of styles, the constant surprises offered to the visitors of the great cities of the world put to shame even the more daring and visionary planners, who can only produce the Brasilias and Canberras of the world.

Economic planners truly believe that what they have learned from the past will be useful in the future and have no hesitation in advising governments of what should be done to make the past happen again!

In reality, the economic process is exactly that, a process, and it is as unfathomable as our individual lives. Are we going to be hit by a car tomorrow? Are terrorists to explode a nuclear device in the heart of London? To say that we can plan for our future is a fallacy; any such claims should always carry the disclaimer that our plan is not for real. It is a very short-term possible scenario for one of the many possible futures in front of us.

The challenge for planners is to plan for freedom, in other words to plan to make things possible, to plan for flexibility, for reorganizing, restructuring, and reconsidering. They should plan to have flexible planning regulations. Plan to make changes in planning possible and finally plan to be surprised.

114

For many years now a very trite strategy has been adopted in economic development. Called SWOT, this strategy is based on preparing a strategic plan by analyzing and appraising the strengths, weaknesses, opportunities, and threats pertaining to the community under scrutiny. In many cases, the process of formulating the strategic plan, instead of being seen as a diagnostic process, that is, an assessment of what is wrong with a patient, is confused with the therapy itself, that is, it is believed to be the cure for the economic ills of the region. In reality, money and time spent in producing a glossy catalogue of intentions and opportunities is basically money spent in producing a book with very limited circulation, with inbuilt obsolescence and very little use. Let's call it a waste of time and space.

This is because to make a plan without having the will or the power to carry it through is futile. For governments to encourage cities and rural communities to carry out extensive planning exercises under the assumption that it will help them can be described as either naive or dishonest. Without the power to implement local resolutions, what is the use of local planning? In centralized systems of government where taxes are collected and administered by state agencies, how can rural communities transform their dreams into reality?

My main objection to wishful planning, however, relates to those who eventually do the planning. In my experience, so-called community planning is done by a fraction of the local inhabitants. Usually these are what I refer to as local aristocrats, that is, the people with either money or time to spare.

It should be noted here that successful business people don't automatically make good public policy makers and that do-gooders with plenty of time to spare don't have the monopoly on wisdom. With rare exceptions, the strategic planning done by such groups is unimaginative, reflective of local prejudices, and likely to emphasize the "unique" aspects of the local community in a self-congratulatory rhetoric.

Once finished, the five- or fifty-year plan becomes a monument to good intentions and a blueprint intended to inspire locals and visitors alike. But what happens to all those good intentions after a few months? Exhausted by the effort to produce "The Plan," weary committee members start to drop out of the working parties.

115

Meanwhile, various letters sent to government departments seeking funds for identified priority projects are written, and the replies come back in a demoralizing trickle. They are all bureaucratic stonewalling, full of the message being that the government will not provide the funds.

After a few years, the once beautifully produced and publicized plan for the development of the city/region is gathering dust, an embarrassing reminder of all the things that should have been and never were.

Is there any value at all in planning? I strongly believe that planning has its role in creating the infrastructures that facilitate the development and growth of a community. Without public utilities and communications, it would be very difficult for individuals and companies to even think about initiating an activity. However the balance between planning for people to be able to take an initiative and planning to destroy initiative is difficult to achieve.

In the town of Esperance, for instance, it was impossible to locate industrial land by the ocean and serviced with power and roads. Nobody in the town planning department had considered the possibility of a group of fishermen ever wishing to invest in an aquaculture plant which required clean, deep ocean water, unpolluted air, and a large power intake to circulate the water.

Maybe when the town's plan was originally done, aquaculture was unheard of, but this is exactly what happens in planning ... nobody can predict what will be required in the future and to make these plans hard to change is ultimately not in the best interests of future generations.

I don't know whether this is true, but I read that in 1860 a group of futurologists was asked to predict how New York City would look in 100 years. They all agreed that by 1960, New York City would not exist because to move the population of that city would have required six million horses, and the manure of six million horses would have created such a problem that the city would have had to have been abandoned!

Schumacher wrote that we don't have a machine to foretell the future. Unfortunately, we have computers and sophisticated planning programs based on present trends which can modify the future, often worsening the situation, as in the case of highways that were planned to ease traffic and ended up encouraging further use of cars, finally worsening congestion.

Life cycles are not linear but complex systems regenerating themselves, taking unpredictable turns, and appearing orderly only at a statistical level. The challenge therefore is truly to thrive on complexity, to accept that chaos is indeed the reason for the existence of the world as we know it.

Planners should ask themselves these questions: Can we plan for freedom? Can we increase the chances for activity, initiative, and genius to occur? If the answer is no, then they should seriously consider whether their role is of any benefit to their communities and evaluate their work accordingly.

Providing infrastructures for development

We have to provide industry and entrepreneurs with physical infrastructures and competent services to allow them to invest in new export and import substitution industries. The price of energy has to become competitive, industrial land has to be provided, transport and microeconomic reform is needed.

The development of an economic system that relies on many more products and services being exported will require the bureaucracy to become more responsive to individual requests for information and advice. It will be harder for government agencies to plan and specialize simply because many more players will be encouraged to find niche markets and to exploit them. Government agencies will have to become more flexible and be prepared to research and facilitate as well as to plan and target new areas of growth.

But this book is essentially about people — passionate people, and passionate people are always innovators and entrepreneurs. Whether involved in economic or social pursuits, they do things because of deep-seated beliefs that often have more to do with their personal value systems than with balance sheets.

Entrepreneurs, both social and economic, are "irrational" people who do what they do not because they seek comfortable, secure, predictable lives, but because they are propelled by inner feelings that make them take action. Such feelings could be love — for the environment, boats, cars, stargazing, or storytelling — hatred or for routine, security without excitement, comfort without romance, and normalcy without adventure.

117

Economic development is only one of the many developments a passionate culture brings forth. Helping people to grow, facilitating the transformation of dreams into rewarding work should not therefore be limited to the economic field but be seen for what it really is: a way of bringing forward change in our society by directly tapping into the source of innovation and energy.

Every area of human endeavor can benefit from increased participation. What Konosuke Matsushita said in a famous speech about industrial practices should therefore be read in a broader context:

> We are going to win and the industrial west is going to lose out. There's nothing much you can do about it, because the reasons for your failure are within yourselves.
>
> Your firms are built on the Taylor model; even worse, so are your heads. With your bosses doing the thinking while the workers wield the screwdrivers, you're convinced deep down that this is the right way to run a business.
>
> For you, the essence of management is getting the ideas out of the heads of the bosses into the hands of labor.
>
> We are beyond the Taylor model. Business, we know, is now so complex and difficult, the survival of the firms so hazardous in an environment increasingly unpredictable, competitive, and fraught with danger that their continued existence depends on the day-to-day mobilization of every ounce of intelligence.

For us, the core of management is precisely this art of mobilizing and pulling together the intellectual resources of all employees in the service of the firm. Because we have measured better than you the scope of the new technological and economic challenges, we know that the intelligence of a handful of technocrats, however brilliant and smart they may be, is no longer enough to take them up with a real chance of success.

Only by drawing on the combined brain power of all its employees can a firm face up to the turbulence and constraints of today's environment.[5]

Shouldn't social and political scientists expound the same creed? Instead of training elites, promoting technocrats, and perpetuating hierarchical systems, shouldn't we learn how to "mobilize every ounce of intelligence?"

It seems extraordinary that the most profound teaching of Dr. Edward Deming, now incarnated in total quality management theory, still escapes the social scientists: You cannot run the company from the top anymore!

Every political system is still firmly a top-down system. The fact that what really makes the world go round are millions of individuals going about their lives the best they can escapes the technocrats, politicians, and bureaucrats who still believe they have a mandate and the skills to "run the firm."

If running a company is very difficult and requires the "combined brain power of all its employees," then running a country is immensely more complex and should, by reason, draw on the talents of all who can contribute. For the nation/firm to prosper, as indicated earlier, the individual quality of all citizens has to improve and come into play. Individual talents have to be treasured and built upon, skills have to match passions, and diversity and participation have to be encouraged.

Facilitation is a way of achieving these aims.

It should be understood and encouraged as a viable strategy in such diverse fields as education, counseling, health delivery services, community, economic, and social development.

By facilitation, however, I mean, one-to-one confidential client-based work. Unfortunately, and inevitably, the term "facilitation" has been used to describe all sorts of activities. The following chapter refers exclusively to person-centered, client-centered approaches starting with the description of facilitation in therapy as applied by the founder of Person-Centered Therapy: Carl Rogers.

12. A Quiet Revolution

"I've had a role in initiating the person-centered approach; this view developed first in counseling and psychotherapy, where it was known as client-centered, meaning a person seeking help was not treated as a dependent patient but as a responsible client. Extended to education, it was called student-centered teaching. As it has moved into a wide variety of fields, far from its point of origin ... it seems best to adopt as broad a term as possible: person-centered."

— Carl Rogers[1]

WHAT OUR SOCIETY STILL COMMONLY DENIES TO MATURE, HEALTHY people, Rogers gave to clients who were, at times, very ill: neurotics, even psychotics. He gave them respect and dignity by treating them as unique human beings.

Whilst in our hospital system, for instance, we still refer to patients by their ailments, for example "a cesarean in room three," Rogers began in the late 1930s to have serious doubts about seeing clients as complex objects, as machines "whose functions may be in disrepair in certain ways." Instead, he became increasingly fascinated by the immense healing powers individuals have, to the point when, after years of practice, he was able to say:

"Therapy is not a matter of doing something to the individual, or to induce him to do something about himself. It is instead a matter of freeing him for normal growth and development, of removing obstacles so that he can again move forward."[2]

Rogers developed facilitative psychological techniques which outraged the establishment by demonstrating two things: first, that the counselor wasn't competent to control the lives of his clients, and second, that the client was best left free to become a self-directing, independent person.

Rogers became famous for his interviews during which he often said nothing — he sat there, attentive, caring, waiting for the client to say something, anything. He would sometimes respond to a statement with a question, drawing the client gently out. No expert, no authority, no instant solution to the client's problem. By being silent, Rogers obliged the client to take action, to stop being a spectator, an infant, a passive, sickly individual waiting to be cured.

He would do the same during week-long seminars for counselors. He would say nothing for days until people would stop looking up to him for solutions and take responsibility for the proceedings, including topics to be discussed, schedule of events, fees, and lunch breaks.Out of the anger, loss and confusion, out of the chaos came — order.

Without a leader, people always organize themselves, without a doctor, they cure each other, without parents they become very quickly adults and fend for themselves.

Parents have the problem of knowing when they can safely let go of their children. Will they be able to fly? Or will they come tumbling down from the nest? Rogers' approach is based on the same belief in the intrinsic goodness of human nature of which Maslow spoke. Rogers wrote:

> Biologists, neuro-physiologists and other scientists, including psychologists, have evidence that adds up to one conclusion. There is in every organism, at whatever level, an underlying flow of movement towards constructive fulfillment of its inherent possibilities. There is a natural tendency towards complete development in man. The term that has most often been used for this is the actualizing tendency, and it is present in all living organisms. It is the foundation on which the person-centered approach is built.[3]

In his work, Rogers demonstrated that even individuals whose conditions were horrible, who were thwarted and blocked from expressing their natural actualizing tendency, still possessed the ability to get back on the path to growth, once the conditions improved.

Facilitators cannot succeed in their work without this fundamental belief in human nature, this faith in the ability of all people to grow to full maturity and to become good people.

To be a facilitator is to be, as Rogers put it, a quiet revolutionary.

At first Roger wasn't aware of the political implications of his work, but he soon realized that he was challenging the very foundations upon which our social system is based. He wrote:

> It is obvious that even this premise of client-centered therapy, without going further, has enormous political implications. Our educational system, our industrial and military organizations, and many other aspects of our culture take the view that the nature of the individual is such that he cannot be trusted — that he must be guided, instructed, rewarded, punished, and controlled by those who are wiser or higher in status. To be sure, we give lip service to a democratic philosophy in which all power is vested in the people, but the philosophy is "honored more in the breach" than in the observance.[4]

121

Facilitators soon realize that their work goes against the grain of conventional wisdom and traditional values. The institutions, agencies, and corporations that theoretically are there to "serve" the public, often do so in an autocratic way. Even churches, aid agencies, and alternative groups such as environmentalists, feminists, gays, and minority and civil rights groups have problems escaping the hierarchical system of organization which they so vehemently reject.

These groups have found that they can go in a short time from revolutionary unstructured groups to paternalistic organizations, that the archetype of the "patron" and the "pater" is so entrenched in the way we organize ourselves that it is nearly impossible to conceive a different system. It seems impossible to run even a preschool meeting without electing a chairperson to run it. And what does the "chair" symbolize if not the throne of the feudal lord? Soon even the preschool committee has abdicated more and more responsibility to the "chair," and parents, without even noticing it, become first silent, then invisible, then a nuisance.

We trust each other so little that we take refuge in leadership — as if an individual charged with the authority to "govern" us would, all of a sudden, become infallible, the water for us, lead us to salvation.

Rogers' refusal to play the chairman's role at conferences created outrage at first — then after a few days the participants would realize what he had done for them. He had shown them that they too could part the waters and lead themselves to salvation. He had shown them that a leader is not necessary when you realize how strong, valuable, wise, and compassionate, in a word, how *good*, your fellow human beings are.

Facilitating education

> "We set out to make a school in which we should allow children freedom
> to be themselves. In order to do this, we had to renounce all discipline,
> all direction, all suggestion, all moral training, all religious instruction ...
> We have been called brave, but it did not require courage. All it required
> was what we had — a complete belief in the child as a good, not an evil,
> being."
>
> —A.S. Neill[5]

How much easier it is to accept the statement that human nature is intrinsically good than to accept A.S. Neill's statement on children's goodness. Every parent, every day, is confronted with the dilemma: to punish or not to punish?

So much energy has gone into searching for answers to the ancient question: "How do we make our children better than we are?" To make them better, we usually beat the psychological life out of them and then lament the consequences. No mater how readily we accept the "intrinsic" goodness of the human race, when it comes to children, we revert to the belief that "goodness" has to be taught to them — and that knowledge has to be poured into that empty vessel that is the child's brain.

The temptation is too strong not to do it. With few exceptions, namely the saints and heroes who inhabit alternative education literature, even the smartest parents among us fall into the trap of believing that without "education" our little treasures would become obnoxious brats, failures, and even antisocial beings, dangerous to themselves and to society.

Yet often we resent what was done to us by our parents, teachers, preachers, and assorted figures of authority. Some of us had to free ourselves from the nightmares, the anxiety, fears, and even boredom which "education" bred into our hearts before we could start our real growth towards maturity and responsibility.

Hope, I believe, can come from a better understanding of children. It seems incredible, for instance, that Sigmund Freud would write that children have to be encouraged to grow, that their natural tendency is to cling to their mothers, to be wanting the comfort of the womb.

If this is true of sick children, it is definitely untrue of healthy ones. Every parent will tell that children delight in growing — that once they learn to crawl they will never be still, that when they learn to walk they will start to climb and joyfully tumble their way from one difficulty to another without us ever having to encourage them.

It is their own wish to grow which propels them. They would walk even if brought up by impaired people. Growth psychologists are encouraging us to consider children as less dependent than previously thought, and to physically and metaphorically unbind our babies.

123▶

Can parenting be more of a guiding than a character-forming activity? The literature on this subject is vast. For the purpose and scope of this book, I would like to suggest that facilitation can be used in educating the young if only we accept that no matter how young, the person we deal with deserves respect.

What education?

David Hilbert, the greatest mathematician of his era, remarked: "Do you know why Einstein said the most original and profound things about space and time that have been said in our generation? Because he had learned nothing about all of the philosophy and mathematics of time and space."

"Educatio," the Latin root of the word "education," meant the teaching of social mores. It was a mothering term and was applied to babies, puppies, and the little ones of all species .... "Educare," for the Latin, had therefore more to do with toilet training than with learning letters, and "rearing" is the best English translation of the word. Even today in modern Italian, "educazione" refers to social skills, to being polite, not learned. The Latin, distinguished between the responsibility of rearing (educare) which was carried out by mothers and nannies and the responsibility of teaching skills (instruire) carried out by skilled adults: master craftspeople and artists.

It seems, however, that we don't distinguish anymore between educating and instructing. Ivan Illich in one of his books makes the point that what we tend to do under the guise of mass education is to treat young adults as babies, extending their "mothering" far beyond what they require and will tolerate.

Witnessing the frustration, anger, even violence occurring in our high schools, I often wonder at the insanity of attempting to "mother" a six-foot-two, one-hundred-and-twenty-kilo seventeen-year-old, who is probably a front row forward in the rugby team! He doesn't need "educatio," to be told what is good for him; he needs "instructio," to learn skills, if possible from professionals who are so good that he can respect them, look up to them, and imitate them.

The main difference I see between the two activities is one of responsibility for the learning. In educating children, we — parents, teachers, nannies — assume the responsibility for the outcome. In other words, the child doesn't ask us to please explain how a gas stove works, or whether it is good manners to put a finger up their nose while being addressed by their great aunt. We take the initiative, we tell them, whether they like it or not. We toilet train them because the consequences of not doing so are too inconvenient.

The justification for educating children is found in the inescapable fact that ours is a social species and that in order to be accepted and to have interaction with others, we have to be able to respect some basic social mores.

I said "basic social mores" because we could easily be carried away by Victorian etiquette and send our children to "finishing schools." This could achieve the opposite result of the one we had set out to achieve. Instead of our children being able to socialize and interact easily with the rest of the species, they may be adept at doing so only with a very limited number of people coming from the same schools and belonging to the same clubs.

A rule of thumb to check on our children's education should be their ability to communicate, to be accepted by and to accept people from different culture — if they can quickly adapt to different social rules and respect others, then they are well-educated.

Puberty

In *The Hero with a Thousand Faces,* Joseph Campbell wrote:

> The so-called rites of passage which occupy such prominent place in the life of primitive society (ceremony of birth, naming, puberty, marriage, burial, etc.) are distinguished by formal and usually very severe exercises of severance, whereby the mind is radically cut away from attitudes, attachments, and the life patterns of the stage left behind.[6]

Puberty seems the appropriate time to stop educating and start instructing. The time comes when children are not ours anymore. In the words of Kahlil Gibran, "they are arrows to our bows."[7]

I don't believe, however, that they are arrows when they are still suckling at the breast, nor when they are still crawling. They would not go far away if shot from our bows then. After puberty yes, they are young adults whether we think so or not. The proof is that they can conceive and give birth; we can deny them their intellectual maturity, but how can we deny their physical maturity?

What are initiation rites but the often-dramatic sign that childhood is ended and responsibility started?

The terror of getting initiated is in the severing from the mother and the beginning of life as an adult. Puberty is the beginning of responsibility and, leaving aside the trauma and the pain that some ceremonies arouse, it has to be said that many "primitive" societies achieve in days what our society struggles to do in years: conferring on the young the status and recognition of adulthood.

Dignity cannot be given to us, nor freedom, nor the sense of fulfillment which is the result of achievement. Adulthood has to be achieved and our deeds become an increasingly important part of the process. Games and "make believe" give way to real action. Skills become a valuable commodity. To be good, whether at dunking a basketball or organizing a party or fixing a motorbike engine, can be the difference between being popular or not.

The switch in responsibility from being educated to learning can only occur when the young realize that they have become young adults and very soon they will have to fend for themselves.

Adolescents desperately need to excel. This fact seems to escape their parents who think that their "children" are still only playing. They aren't. They are proving themselves to the "world" by becoming the best, whether at surfing, computer games or looking "cool."

The fact that the skills which appeal to teenagers are different from those which appeal to their elders should never cloud the real issue that adolescents are eager to learn and that they should be given the opportunity to do so.

What would happen if "education" would ease into "instruction" in the years immediately following puberty? What would happen if students could determine what they wished to learn according to their age? And what would happen if students could choose to learn from professionals and not teachers?

Probably what would happen would be the demystification of the education system as we know it, because students would soon find out that formal education doesn't hold the key to success in life. They would discover that out there are people who are happy and unhappy, rich and poor, fulfilled and unfilled no matter what their academic qualifications are. They would also discover that the great majority of individuals resent what was imposed on them during their years of formal schooling and tend to say that they have learned more on the job and by themselves than at school.

In an article entitled "Things I wish I had known at 18," Roald Dahl writes:

> But I was convinced, even at eighteen and still am, that University is an absolute load of old rubbish unless you go into a profession. People say it's a marvelous opportunity to take stock and mature, but you can bloody well mature by getting a job, working like hell, and steaming around the place.

The point is that we can learn exciting and profitable skills outside the formal education system — since all education, in the end, is self-education. This is because the brain cannot cope with the billions of items of information reaching it. Out of everything which is available, we pick what is of interest, what is relevant to us. We may read the same book, yet we may remember even be brought to tears by completely different parts of it. One may love it, another be indifferent to it.

Reality, as some philosophers say, may be the same for all of us — the fact is that we perceive it through our senses and process it through our brain. The interpretation of identical experiences may therefore be very different.

Formal education is based on the assumption that information and knowledge may be imparted, that a good teacher is able to make students absorb and comprehend what has been taught. The quality of those who receive the message, however, is as important as the quality of the teacher in making the exchange of information possible. It is like broadcasting a radio message at a frequency that is too high or too low for the receiver to pick up. No matter how good the broadcast is, nothing will be received.

This explains why words of immense wisdom spoken by the most sublime masters have failed to change the world. It is not that the masters couldn't convince us ... rather, that we simply didn't get the message. We heard the words but we missed the meaning.

127

The fact is that we can only pick what we understand, only what interests us ... or maybe it is the other way around: we become interested only in what we understand. Like children who love swimming because they are good at it, so we too use our natural buoyancy to excel in doing what we naturally are well versed in.

A well-educated child who can read, write, and communicate should by puberty be encouraged to seek responsibility for his/her further studies, including the acquisition of skills with ever-increasing independence. The search for skills coincides with a search for individuality and recognition, and adolescence is the best time to try, to strive, and to find out what it is that you love doing.

What happens, however, is that adolescents are eager to learn only skills that are relevant to them. Sometimes the skills provided by the formal education system are relevant to them, sometimes they are not. What happens when they aren't?

Mass education is like a dream gone wrong. The dream may very well have been for every child to become a professional ... the nightmare is what we are left with after the artists, the inventors, the lateral thinkers, the manual workers, and nearly all of the entrepreneurs are forced through a system they utterly despise.

What would happen if at puberty, "education" eased into self-determined "instruction"? Could we trust young adults enough to allow them to determine what they want to grab hold of and when? Ivan Illich wrote:

> A good education system should have three purposes: It should provide all who want to learn with access to available resources at any time in their lives; empower all who want to share what they know to find those who want to learn it from them; and, finally, furnish all who want to present an issue to the public with the opportunity to make their challenge known.[8]

Clearly, the "good education system" of which Illich speaks couldn't exist without the belief that firstly, people want to learn, and secondly, they know what they wish to learn.

128 Facilitation, the person-centered approach which is the topic of this book, is based on similar assumptions: transferred to the education system, it means that no matter how good the outcome of a formal education system is, what self-educated individuals will create will be immensely more valuable. This is because the richness is with people, not with systems; with the exception, not the norm; with chaos not with order. To quote Einstein, "imagination is more important than knowledge."

Children who have been properly "educated," that is, children who can communicate, accept, and be accepted by the world's community will naturally and effortlessly mature into responsible adults. They will eagerly seek instruction because it is their nature to do so, not because we oblige them to. As a society, we would be better off trusting them rather than trying to achieve the impossible dream of the planners and bureaucrats.

The master — the teacher

> "Only those who are eager to learn do I instruct."
> —Confucius[9]

Teachers assume the responsibility to educate. The students' only responsibility is to carry their physical body to the classroom — they don't even need to pay attention, the teacher will attract it! Every day sees new tricks, an education aid, a video, a gimmick. The children are in a passive learning situation.

Masters, however, don't care about motivating the pupils. They are too busy making a living to be concerned about it. The responsibility for learning is squarely on the shoulders of the pupils. If they don't pay attention, if they don't come to work, it's too bad for them.

Adolescents need masters, not teachers. The anger, frustration, boredom, and violence so prevalent in our secondary schools could be avoided by providing, on demand, the best possible instructor to each pupil. Some of these instructors will be found among the ranks of the formally educated, that is teachers and professionals, some among business people, artists, and sports people. The formal school could be used as the place where you meet with the facilitators who will help you shape your own unique path towards personal and professional fulfillment.

A friend of mine went to a university a few years ago and asked to be allowed to attend three different courses in Horse Husbandry (run by the Faculty of Veterinary Studies,) in Business, and in Marketing (run by the Faculty of Economics). He explained that he only wanted to learn and that he didn't want any certificate or recognition for his attendance.

129

He was laughed out of the Registrar's office — not only didn't he have the qualifications to enter veterinary studies, even if he did, there would have been no way he would have been allowed to attend only Horse Husbandry. Business and Marketing were out of the question, and the idea of doing one unit here and another there was considered unthinkable.

My friend at the time was managing a "Gypsy Caravan Park," a very successful tourist and holiday attraction for people to drive their self-contained horse-drawn caravan through the forests of Western Australia. The skills he needed were horse husbandry, business, and marketing. He was right in his choice of courses but the university was clearly inadequate or unwilling to help him.

How many cases are there where legitimate, intelligent, profitable activities "invented" by lateral thinkers and entrepreneurs don't find any response at the level of formal education?

There is no correlation that I can find between schooling and entrepreneurial skill. The only association is a negative one, brutally exemplified in the title of Robert T. Kiyosaki's book *If You Want to be Rich and Happy Don't Go to School!* I have yet to find an entrepreneur who was encouraged to pursue self-employment by a teacher. Could it be that teachers are terrified of the new and unstructured? Of something that does not appear in any book? Could it be that they honestly believe that their pupils will fail in life if they don't pass mathematics or geography?

I know a number of migrants who came to Australia in the 1950s with hardly a cent in their pockets, no formal education, and not a word of English. Some of them still can't write, but that hasn't stopped them from becoming millionaires.

Keith Bradby, the self-educated botanist and environmentalist, ministerial advisor and author, once answered a questionnaire in which he was required to describe his educational background. Under the heading "EDUCATION" he wrote: "Yes — briefly interrupted by two years of formal schooling"!

130 Belief in people's intrinsic wish to grow allows for a change in attitude towards education. The delivery of the national curriculum would be tempered by a degree of responsiveness not seen in today's schools. Individual even idiosyncratic needs would be encouraged, and students would be helped to find masters outside the formal school setting, who could provide the skills they require.

Teachers, I believe, would rather see their students spending two or three days a week working at something they love doing than sitting bored and despondent in their classrooms. Opening the formal education system to outsiders by sending students to learn from professionals presents its challenges , however. The remuneration of the skill-providers would have to come from the education budget on a pro rata basis. The credentials of the professionals involved would have to be checked. In my opinion, these and probably many other administrative and logistical problems pale to insignificance, when compared with the absurdity and waste of forcing the same curriculum on vastly different people.

From an economic point of view, it is important that educators realize that the so-called "nonacademically gifted" students who now fall between the cracks of the education system are as important and precious to the nation as those who will get their higher education certificates. The majority of tomorrow's entrepreneurs will probably come from the ranks of the former. They will employ the accountants, engineers, and business school graduates puoduced by the formal education system.

All over the world, small business is the engine which runs the economy; certainly it is the sector which creates the majority of jobs. Wouldn't it be appropriate to provide those who wish to run Gypsy Caravan Parks, for example, the skills required for doing so more efficiently? The idea of providing students with education vouchers is not new but could be a flexible method of developing an individual and self-directed type of education.

Maybe secondary school students could be given an increasingly larger number of vouchers every year. Such vouchers would be redeemable not only when attending formal school but also when working with professionals — business people, artists, and skilled individuals prepared to pass on their trade. To qualify to accept and cash in a voucher, the instructor would have to submit to the education department a resume indicating a history of experience. Such a system would allow the **131** carpenter, writer, film director, mechanic, etc. to be a master once again and to participate in teaching skills to the young. Those who have experienced what happens when people wishing to learn a skill are exposed to masters of their trade will agree with me that we should do whatever is in our power to multiply such opportunities.

Nothing tastes sweeter than water to those who are thirsty; nothing will ever be learned faster than something that truly interests us.

A society which makes it easy for people to learn what they wish to learn will be a society enormously richer than one whose education has been engineered by bureaucrats and statisticians.

Ultimately the message is the same, whether dealing with educational, society or economic issues: there is wisdom at the grassroots level, which cannot be understood by dissecting it.

Living organisms and the human race in particular, are extremely complex and seem to react in unpredictable ways to the attempts at management by well-intentioned planners.

Going with the energy of individual people requires a shift from having expectations about outcomes to rediscovering faith. The way things are in education seems out of step with what is really needed to regenerate a creative spirit in the young. The world is changing rapidly; education lags sadly behind.

13. The Politics of Personal Growth

"Our politics, like our psychology, has lost touch with the concept of human health. We think mainly in terms of acute social ailments and first aid remedies, rarely in terms of the fullest possibilities of human growth and how societies may facilitate it."

— Walt Anderson[1]

CAN WE MAKE OUR INSTITUTIONS RESPONSIVE TO INDIVIDUAL NEEDS?

Yes.

The best of the local Enterprise Facilitation programs set up in Australia and in New Zealand are an example of organizations which only respond to individual requests and resist the temptation of deciding what is good for people and pushing it down their throats. But it has taken an almighty effort to achieve a minuscule step in changing existing institutions from deciding what is good for you and me to helping us achieve whatever it is we wish to achieve.

This has required an ideological shift, and we need our political system to keep in step with this approach. We need a political system based on human values and human development.

Currently, our social institutions are based on a behaviorist model, which reflects the belief that human nature cannot be trusted and human behavior must be controlled. J.B. Watson, the best-known early spokesperson for the behaviorist movement in America, said that the behaviorist "would like to develop his world of people from birth on, so that their speech and bodily behavior could equally well be exhibited freely everywhere without running afoul of group standards."[2] Social engineering is the ultimate aim of the behaviorist who argues, like B.F. Skinner, that "the only difference I expect to see revealed between the behavior of rat and man (aside from enormous differences of complexity) lies in the field of verbal behavior."[3] Very complex talking "rats" is as different a definition of the human race as one could find from the hopeful image painted by Maslow and Rogers.

And the tools for achieving control are, for the behaviorist, conditioning by means of positive and/or negative reinforcement. Reward and punishment are the techniques. Donald Baer, who studied such techniques, has come to the following conclusion:

133

> "In general, behaviorists have found punishment to be one of the fastest and most effective techniques for helping people rid themselves of troublesome behavior."[4]

The ideas of the behaviorists have influenced and permeated our society. According to Edwin Boring, an eminent historian of psychology, "for a while, in the 1920s, it seemed as if all America had gone behaviorist."[5] These methods are still with us. Behavioristic Political Science is well known for ignoring aspects of human behavior which are "emotional," "subjective," "personal" — in other words, all that is pertinent to me and you as unique individuals and members of the community.

Social engineering, the statistical perception of society, the tax numbers, the computerized medical and credit practices, and the violations of our dignity and freedom are only initial steps towards the fulfillment of the behaviorists' dream so clearly presented by Skinner:

> We can achieve a sort of control under which the controlled though they are following a code much more scrupulously than was ever the case under the old system, nevertheless feel free.[6]

The mind shudders at the thought of who would be in charge of such "perfect" conditioning. Who would control the controllers? This is nothing short of the nightmare described in Orwell's *1984*. Fortunately, those in charge of our bureaucracy have not been given Skinner's mandate, nor they have mastered the techniques necessary to achieve such control over us. Hopefully we are — and don't just feel free.

It is true, however, that institutions tend to create programs based on statistical truths, on percentages, aggregates, and mathematical formulas. Their programs therefore seems to address "people" (generic noun), never individuals (singular spirited human beings, of flesh and blood). If you are not smack in the middle of the statistical curve, then you don't fit the program. All of a sudden you are not "people" anymore. The institution, which is there to assist "people," doesn't consider you "people" and you are expected to disappear.

Even the more benign organizations can get so carried away designing the perfect plan to create the perfect world that they can become impatient with people interrupting them. "Here we are," they seem to say, "designing the perfect world, and all these stupid people ring in with their pathetic requests!"

The Italian poet Gioacchino Belli wrote a poem titled "La Statistica" which roughly translates as "Statistics is the science which says that if I have eaten two chickens and you none, then we have eaten a chicken each!" We should be very skeptical of "experts" who only use mathematical data to create images of the perfect society and then try to build Utopia with total disregard for our immediate needs, which include freedom, dignity, and self-respect. Their zeal has to be tempered by the realization that ultimately society is not an abstract entity, but a conglomerate of individuals. Only the improvement of each of them will result in a better society. Paradoxically, manipulation, coercion and mind control, will achieve the opposite result.

The bureaucrat as a facilitator

> "Our new vision of the possibilities of human existence becomes a set of guidelines for building a human community; it is no longer the concern merely of writers and clinicians and social scientists but a res publica, a public thing."
>
> —Walt Anderson[7]

Many minorities and civil liberties groups are screaming it every day: "Stop patronizing us, stop pushing us around, stop deciding what is good for us and administering it whether we like it or not!" "Experts" are no longer trusted without question. We want to know why we should take a certain action. We have the right to ask questions and get answers.

My father, a medical practitioner, tells me that once he could recommend a treatment to a patient and be implicitly trusted and obeyed. He says: "Nowadays, the patients want to know why they should take a particular drug, what's in it, what the alternative is, and then they will go to another doctor to get a second opinion."

Authority, I believe, can only survive in an ignorant environment. The more the population educates itself, the harder it will become to force anything upon it. The problem faced by today's bureaucracy is that it struggles to meet the demands that an increased social awareness brings forth. Examples would be an agriculture department being successfully sued by a group of farmers because their cattle became contaminated following the compulsory spraying of a pesticide, or psychiatric patients taking successful action against the health department which allowed questionable treatment.

Bureaucrats will increasingly think more carefully about imposing anything on anybody. Once public servants were among the few literates; like the scribes and tax collectors of ancient times, they were perceived as being very close to the source of power and able to impose their decisions because of their close connection with the executive. Fascist and communist bureaucracies have been ruthless in enforcing the demands of their ideologies — and in provoking, with their corruption and pettiness, the collapse of the very system that supported them.

Today, more and more people, individuals, the "battlers," are able to take the bureaucracy on and to get some justice. The tide is turning away from authoritarianism in every field. From the corporate world right through to the family bedroom, the trend is towards respect and empowerment and away from enforced discipline and manipulation.

It is inescapable, then, that the bureaucrat of the future can only be a facilitator. The reasons are obvious: intelligent, well-informed people will increasingly scrutinize any action and rules that bureaucrats make. The risk of liability litigation and public ridicule will make it very difficult for any so-called "expert" to administer any "treatment" or program without the full and informed consent of the client. The electronic media with their ability to network are already making it easier for individuals who believe they are the victims of injustice to find others in the same situation and to form lobbies to fight it.

The conservatives believe that minority pressure groups impede the political process by occupying center stage and overshadowing the silent majority. One could argue that, on the contrary, these publicity-conscious, and vocal groups are nothing more than the visible projection of a change in consciousness which is touching all of us, that is, the recognition of the uniqueness and intrinsic value of every being.

No matter how conservative you may be, without a doubt your attitude towards your doctor, lawyer, and public servant has changed in accordance with the emerging consciousness that can be observed in the community. These trends raise important questions: Can we change the bureaucracy from "working for the rulers" to "working for the people?" Can we democratize our institutions to make them responsive to individual needs? Are the "experts," the "planners," the "bureaucrats" forever to decide what is good for you and me?"

Writing about politics, Abraham Maslow made the following observation:

> "No social reforms, no beautiful programs or laws will be of any consequence unless people are healthy enough, evolved enough, strong enough, good enough to understand them and to want to put them into practice in the right way. The good society, is useless ... unless there are relatively good people to implement it, carry it out, and live it through."[8]

The corollary of the above is that good people create a good society even without the development and implementation of a utopian blueprint. Could it be that today's institutions are the reflection of a sick society?

In *Gestalt Therapy*, Perls, Hefferline, and Goodman wrote:

> The prevention of outgoing motion and initiative, the social derogation of aggressive drives, the epidemic increase of self-control and self-conquest have led to a language in which the self seldom does or expresses anything; instead, "it" happens. These restrictive measures have also led to a view of the world as completely neutral and "objective" and unrelated to our concerns; and to institutions that take over our functions, that are to "blame" because they "control" us, and that wreak on us the hostility which we so carefully refrain from wielding ourselves — as if men did not themselves lend to institutions whatever force they have!"[9]

It seems that we build cages around ourselves just to be able to rattle them!

Today, becoming independent from institutions takes on a new significance. Becoming stronger and healthier at a personal level assumes political connotations; in a sense such growth will achieve change without a revolution. There is again: Walt Anderson

> To talk of political revolution as we have known it, becomes irrelevant to our times. Nobody will have to overthrow the state; we will simply outgrow our need for many of its functions.[10]

Maybe one day even the facilitator will be superseded, by what, I don't know, but right now I cannot see how individuals can become all that they possibly can become without finding the resources and information they need to do so.

137

Facilitating people's growth implies therefore a different kind of institution — one which, using Ivan Illich's terminology, we can describe as "convivial" as opposed to "manipulative." Illich's convivial institution is one which is distinguished by the spontaneous use of things such as "telephone link-ups, subway lines, mail routes, public markets ... sewerage systems, drinking water, parks and sidewalks", institutions men use without having to be institutionally convinced that it is to their advantage to do so. "Such institutions," Illich adds, "tend to be networks which *facilitate* [my emphasis] client-initiated communication and co-operation."[11]

Interestingly, recent studies in corporate management see a trend to flexible client-driven project teams which create a human resources package on a job-need basis and which disband at the end of the assignment.

Local enterprise facilitators perform for their clients the same functions as the aforementioned firms, that is they address the clients' requests and endeavor to find suitable people to form a team to help realize their projects. In a sense, Enterprise Facilitators are like family doctors. They only work on demand, that is, they wait for the client/patient to get in touch and, like family doctors, they are general practitioners — they have a good grasp of the whole and refer the client to a specialist if necessary.

Professionals such as doctors, lawyers, accountants, and others don't need to convince the public to use their services. In this regard, they are closer to the facilitator's model than even the most socially aware and considerate bureaucrat who has to sell the government scheme of the day and ends up manipulating the "participants."

Can our institutions be remodeled to facilitate people to grow on their own? They would require the services of a new breed of professional bureaucrats who are not only natural people's people, but also trained to listen and respect.

We don't have a name for such people yet. Illich quotes Yevgeny Yevtushenko:

> "We now need a name for those who value hope above expectations. We need a name for those who love people more than products, those who believe that no people are uninteresting, their fate is like the chronicle of planets. Nothing in them is not particular, and planet is dissimilar from planet."[12]

14. Epilogue

Civic Society, Social Capital,
and the Creation of Wealth

"Where the people are not capable of self-government, they are incapable of being governed. While we may reach some intended short-term objectives through forced behavior, it is almost always with substantial, destructive, unforeseen consequences. In such command and control organizations, the intended consequences may or may not happen, the unintended consequences always do."

— Dee Hock[1]

ENTERPRISE FACILITATION WAS BORN OUT OF A DESIRE TO PROVE THE basic tenets of humanistic psychology that people have an intrinsic wish to grow and that they can become better providers, parents, and citizens if only the obstacles in their paths are removed.

After fifteen years of never initiating and never motivating people, we have accumulated ample evidence that people, anywhere, if only given the chance, will come forward with their unique program for self-improvement, their dreams — and they will strive to realize them.

For those who love statistics, 50,000 people contact the 36 trained Enterprise Facilitators in Western Australia every year. In Esperance, in the past eleven years 1,800 people have contacted Brian Willoughby every single year. He has assisted in the creation of 410 new enterprises in a community of 14,000 people without ever initiating a project or attempting to motivate anyone. What more proof do we need that we should rethink behavioristic motivational theory and command-and-control practices?

Robert Putnam's book *Making Democracy Work: Civic Traditions in Modern Italy* offers a 1,000-year account of two regions in Italy, which developed under differing civic conditions. Here is the historical evidence that people who are free to become what they wish to become are, in the long term, better, and better off, than those who have been dominated and controlled.

Putnam, Professor of Government at Harvard University, wrote *Making Democracy Work* after a twenty-year study of the newly introduced regional governments in Italy. The constitutional requirement to introduce regional authorities had been enacted in 1970, and Putnam was interested in finding out how different regions would use self-governance to advance their social, economic, and environmental causes.

In conducting his research Putnam used a multitude of analytical tools, all aimed at exploring the origins of effective government and the link between institutional performance and the character of civic life, which he calls "civic community." Using twelve indicators ranging from legislative output to the availability of day care centers, he discovered that the gaps between the "best" regions of Italy and the "worst" were of such magnitude that they could not be explained by recent economic, geographic, or political factors. For instance, the number of day care centers ranged from one for every 400 children in Italy's best region to one for every 12,560 in the worst, from one family health clinic for every 15,000 residents in the best region to one for every 3,850,000 inhabitants in the worst. Cabinet stability ranged from two cabinets every ten years in the best region, to nine cabinets in ten years in the worst. Putnam writes: "By the 1980s, Emilia-Romagna, with one of the most dynamic economies in the world, was on its way to becoming the wealthiest region in Italy and among the most advanced in Europe, while Calabria was the poorest region in Italy and among the most backward in Europe."[2]

Putnam's inquiry into the reasons for such considerable gaps made him look at the history of some of the regions of Italy, and he discovered that 1,000 years ago the richest and the poorest areas of modern Italy had been equally wealthy. The southern Italian "Kingdom of Two Sicilies" had been the coveted possession of a number of foreign conquerors. Rich in natural resources, including forests and agricultural land, the kingdom extended from the south of Rome all the way to Sicily and Puglia and was by far the largest kingdom on the Italian peninsula. The Emilia-Romagna region, situated in the north-central part of Italy (north of Florence and south of Venice), had beena mostly agricultural area, renowned for its livestock markets and silk weaving.

During the Middle Ages the GNP of the two areas was comparable yet the way the wealth was owned, generated and distributed differed considerably. The southern Italian kingdom was ruled autocratically and all resources were the property of the feudal lord. The great majority of the region's inhabitants were impoverished peasants who worked the feudal land with no hope of ever becoming landowners. Emilia-Romagna, on the other hand, was dominated by city-states and communal republics, which **141** required the cooperation of all citizens for administration and defense. Free men owned land, organized their farmers' markets and sat as equals to the local aristocracy on city councils. Merchants and farmers administered the "borgo"; they were the ancestors of the bourgeoisie which established the first universities and banks in Europe and gave us the Renaissance.

What happened in 1,000 years to the wealth of Southern Italy? The symbol for this decline may well be Castel Del Monte, the beautiful octagonal castle that Frederick II built in Puglia to hunt venison in the surrounding dense forest. The castle now stands in a barren desert of eroded land. The trees are long gone, even the soil has been mined, and no wealth remains. Putnam has this to say about the qualities of that region's citizenry:

> The very concept of citizenship is stunted there. Engagement in social and cultural associations is meager. From the point of view of the inhabitants, public affairs is somebody else's business — *I notabili*, "the bosses'," "the politicians'", but not theirs.[3]

The result is diffidence and a resigned fatalism about one's life, the state of the economy, and the possibilities for improvement. Southern Italy is now famous, or should we say infamous, for car bombings of anti-Mafia judges, for corruption in public administration, and for unemployment rates which top sixty percent in some of the cities.

Regions in the North, however, "have many active community organizations. Citizens in these regions are engaged by public issues, not by patronage, they trust one another to act fairly and to obey the law. Social and political networks are organized horizontally, not hierarchically. These 'civic communities' value solidarity, civic participation, and integrity. And here democracy works."[4]

Emilia-Romagna, a region of four million people, boasts one business for every eleven people, and ninety percent of those businesses have fewer than ninety-nine workers. In Carpi, the knitwear capital of Europe, there are 2,500 companies that generate a turnover of $2 billion per year. What is remarkable is that the community only has 60,000 people and that the average workforce in the local factories numbers five!

Civic leaders have, often with no or only a belated involvement of the government, created industry organizations, cooperatives, and a myriad of other organizations to provide small and medium enterprises with state-of-the-art management and technical advice. Rural credit unions and workers' cooperatives were introduced to the region 100 years ago in response to rural economic and political changes.

One at a time, often championed by a solitary, passionate, and educated individual, cooperatives in the region have grown to number 7,600, of which 2,400 are in the rural sector. Farmers cultivate in a cooperative manner, transform their crops into finished products in their own regional cooperatives, and have participated in the formation of cooperative supermarket chains which are becoming a sizable player in national and European markets.

In Emilia-Romagna civic intelligence is also visible at the local and regional government level, where the lawmakers are often creating initiatives which precede and stimulate national debate and legislation.

Civic economy

"Development economists take note: civic matters."
— Robert Putnam[5]

Economists, certainly in Emilia-Romagna, know this. The Chair of Economics at the university of Bologna calls the Emilia-Romagna model an example of civic economy; he is a very fervent advocate of an economic system which is beyond capitalism, that is, a system which enhances participation in the creation of wealth, not only in its accumulation.

Civic economy can be defined as the economy resulting from generalized reciprocity, from people helping people to succeed, with the understanding that the well-being of each member of the community is to everybody's advantage. Whereas unbridled capitalism destroys diversity, competition, and ultimately the market and has to be controlled with anti-trust laws, civic economy encourages diversity and supports small and medium companies and cooperatives with both legislative and fiscal tools.

The result is an entrepreneurial economy where reciprocity matters. It is essential for entrepreneurs to collaborate, and in Emilia-Romagna, with one company for every eleven people, every family has direct experience of the advantages of cooperation and mutuality.

143

Historically, solidarity and reciprocity in the region were the result of weak, not of strong government:

> In the North during the eleventh century the attempts to revive Imperial power all ended in failure and local particularism triumphed all but completely. It was in this region, stretching from Rome to the Alps, that the characteristic Italian society of the Middle Ages was free to evolve most fully; here the communes became in effect city states, so that the area may be conveniently described as communal Italy.[6]

Looking after their own made citizens out of farmers and merchants, reminding us of the "self interest rightly understood" of which Alexis de Tocqueville wrote in *Democracy in America*. Communal barn raising also comes to mind, and North Americans will be able to draw parallels between the regions of Northern Italy that Putnam describes and the colonization of the West. The West could never have been won without the early pioneers' solidarity, cooperation, and trust in each other. Yet the myth of the rugged individual persists and even informs American political theory, with Liberals stressing individualism and individual rights and Republicans emphasizing community and the obligation of citizenship.

Is there a way of reconciling the two theories and in so doing, explaining, what makes a society civic? Could it be that civic society is the result of *rugged individuals working together* for mutual advantages? Are we sure that individualism and civic values are irreconcilable?

Civic humanism

> "The most dramatic revision of the history of political thought of the last 25 years or so is the discovery and celebration of civic humanism."
> — Don Herzog[7]

Service to others, compassion, concern, empathy, generosity, etc. are not the preserve of saints and heroes. They are daily occurrences that we witness and experience and that remind us of who we are and who we may be.

According to Maslow, healthy human beings who have satisfied basic materialistic needs develop other and higher needs. These new needs are of a psychological, not a material nature, and their satisfaction is as urgent as the former. They are the needs for love, companionship, respect, self-respect, and finally, self-actualization.

If we believe in Maslow's hierarchy of needs, the dichotomy between individualism and community membership vanishes. This is because the individual who is free to become, *becomes* social. In other words, as soon as basic needs are satisfied, people who are free to express their individuality will naturally seek others because only *others* can satisfy their higher needs for love, companionship, respect, etc.

How far individuals can go in expressing and celebrating their inner talents is a measure of the society they live in. The difference between the impoverished peasants of Southern Italy and the impoverished peasants of Northern Italy, in the eleventh century, was not the amount of food they had — it was their ability to dream of a better personal future.

In an autocratic state, under feudal laws, lineage, not intelligence or ability, is the paramount factor determining people's "station" in life. Like overbearing parents who crush their children's ability to grow, the feudal system crushes the ability of people to become citizens. Feudalism, slavery, and apartheid lead to similar results: they stop those who are subject to their rule from becoming all they can become.

Under such regimes people are obliged to restrict their horizons and to only socialize in their ghettos, and their personal ambitions are severely curtailed. In such an environment, the particularly gifted often become the rebels fighting against the system that represses them. Italian popular revolutionary heroes came only from the south; the gifted northern children became city councilors, judges, poets, and artisans!

Thus, the *freedom to become* is the key to unlocking civic society and long-term economic prosperity. Wealth can be generated in the short-term by exploiting natural resources, but 1,000 years of prosperity can only be created intelligently by working together, exchanging ideas, sharing technology and resources, and helping each other to do well in the understanding that a myriad of wealthy self-employed people produces an economic system immensely more resilient than any alternative.

The beauty of Maslow's theory is that it explains that helping each other is not done out of charity, but out of our need to be appreciated, loved, and respected. Healthy individuals, who have fulfilled their materialistic needs, fulfill their higher needs by engaging in convivial activities — those activities which make living together more enjoyable. Such people volunteer, engage in civic activities, and donate to good causes with an abandon that is totally incomprehensible to people still struggling to make ends meet.

American Indian Chiefs knew very well that only by donating all their possession to others could they maintain their status. A society of Chiefs is the precondition for an economy of abundance. Such society is the ideal habitat for strong, smart, even "rugged" individuals.

They will be able to use their amazing skills to save their towns. They will find love in the process, earn the respect of everybody, and, with a bit of luck, be home for lunch just before High Noon!

NOTES

INTRODUCTION

1. J. Moon and K. Willoughby, *Case Studies in Local Development —
The Esperance Experience* (Canberra: Commonwealth Office of
Local Government and the W.A. Department of Regional
Development and the North West, 1988), p. 5.

I. OUT OF AFRICA

The notes for this chapter are not designed to provide full references in
accordance with scholarly conventions. Their main purpose is to indicate
to readers where they might go to pursue some arguments that could only
be made here very briefly.

For a concise introduction to the thought of economic development as it
relates to developing countries, see:

- H.W. Arendt, *Economic Development* (Chicago: University Press, 1987)

For a good introduction to the problematique of development, see the
following:

- A.N. Agarwala and S.P. Singh, eds., *The Economics of Underdevelopment* (New York: Oxford University Press, 1963)

- Gunnar Myrdal, *The Challenge of World Poverty* (New York:
Pantheon, 1970)

- P.T. Bauer, *Dissent on Development* (Cambridge, Mass: Harvard
University Press, 1972)

- Robert Rhodes, ed., *Imperialism and Underdevelopment* (New York:
Monthly Review Press, 1970)

- Jacques Austruy, *Le scandale du développement* (Paris: Marcel
Rivière, 1968)

- Ivan Illich, *Tools for Conviviality* (New York: Harper and Row, 1973)

For a more recent, and conflicting, perspective see:

- Jacques Binet, *Développement. Transfer de technologie. Transfer de
culture* (Paris: Diogène, April-June 1984)

- R.M. Sundrum, *Development, Economics: A Framework for Analysis
and Policy* (London: Wiley, 1983)

- E.F. Schumacher, *Small is Beautiful: Economics as if People Mattered* (New York: Harper & Row, 1973)

2. THE TECHNOLOGICAL FIX

1. See the following:

   - Jackson Report, *Etude de la Capacité du système de Nations Unies pour le Développement* (ONU: Geneve, 1970)

   - Barbara Ward et al., *The Widening Gap: Development in the 1970s* (New York: Columbia University Press, 1971).

   - *Strategia Internazionale dello Sviluppo per il Secondo Decennio delle Nazioni Unite* (Bollettino di Informazioni: UNESCO, n.13, 1971)

2. E.F. Schumacher, *Small is Beautiful*, p. 172.

3. Ibid., p. 249.

147

3. HOMO CUPIENS — the desiring man

1. A.H. Maslow, *Motivation and Personality* (New York: Harper & Row, 1954), p. 201.

2. A.H. Maslow, *Towards a Psychology of Being* (New York: Van Nostrand, 1968), p.5.

3. A.H. Maslow, *Motivation and Personality*, p. 69.

4. Ibid., pp. 69-70.

5. Ibid., pp. 82-83.

6. Ibid., p. 89.

7. Ibid., p. 91.

8. A.H. Maslow, "A Theory of Metamotivation: The Biological Rooting of the Value-Life" (*Journal of Humanistic Psychology* [1967], Vol. VII, No. 2), quoted in Chiang & Maslow, *The Healthy Personality: Readings* (New York: Van Nostrand, 1969).

9. E.F. Schumacher, "Economic Development and Poverty," *Manas*, Vol. 20, Feb. 15, 1967, pp 1-8.

10. Walt Anderson, *Politics and the New Humanism* (Pacific Palisades: Goodyear Publishing Co., 1973), p. 45.

4. OUT OF THE MOUNTAIN CAVE BACK TO SCHOOL

1. A.H. Maslow, *Towards a Psychology of Being*, p. 221.

2. Christian Bay, "The Cheerful Science of Dismal Politics," in *The Dissent Academy*, ed. Theodore Roszak (New York: Random House, 1976), p. 232.

3. For those interested in further readings I suggest the following authors: G. Allport, G. Murphy, J. Moreno, H.A. Murray (Personality Psychologists); A. Adler, O. Rank, C. Jung (New Freudians); F. Perls, R. Hefferline, P. Goodman (Gestaltists); R. Assagiol (Psycho-synthesis).

4. For those interested in the classical humanistic tradition, I suggest the pre-Socratic thinkers (especially Progatoras, Heraclitus, and the Sophists); Pico Della Mirandola, Nicola Abbaganano (Renaissance Humanists); Moses Hadas, *Humanism* (New York: Harper & Brothers, 1960).

5. Carl Rogers, *Carl Rogers on Personal Power* (London: Constable, 1978), p. 6.

7. THE ESPERANCE MODEL APPLIED

1. J. Moon, K. Willoughby, *The Esperance Experience*, pp. 35-36.

2. *Local Economic Development Initiatives — Policy-Coordination and Funding* (W.A., Premiers Department, unpublished government report, 1987).

3. *The Rural Enterprise Victoria Scheme (REV) Guidelines* (Victoria: Department of Agriculture and Rural Affairs, unpublished Government Report, December 1988).

4. *Waimate Plains District Council, Establishment of Local Enterprise Facilitator*, (Manaia, unpublished report, 1988).

5. New Zealand Department of Labor, *Dreams to Reality* (Taranaki, 1991), p. 9.

6. Ibid., p. 8.

8. ON FACILITATION

1. E. Schumacher, *Good Work* (London: Abacus, 1980), p. 65.

2. Quoted in T. Peters, *Liberation Management* (New York: Alfred Knopf, 1992), p. 592.

3. G. Bateson, *Steps to an Ecology of Mind* (Herefordshire, U.K.: Granada, 1973), p. 117.

4. Robert M. Pirsig, *Zen and the Art of Motorcycle Maintenance* (London: Corgi Books, 1976), p. 290.

5. Ibid., p. 291.

9. TRAINING FACILITATORS

1. D.H. Smith, *Confucius* (London: Temple Smith, 1973), Analects IX, p. 18.

2. Lao-tzu, *Tao Te Ching* (Middlesex, U.K.: Penguin, 1963), LV11, 133, p. 118.

3. Paratemia is a brine shrimp used as a feed for tropical fish. It is found in abundance in salt lakes around Esperance and as yet is not utilized commercially. Australia imports a similar shrimp from the U.S.A. in dried form.

4. E. Sirolli, *Enterprise Facilitator Training Manual*, St. Paul: Sirolli Institute, 1997, p. 11.

5. P. Drucker, *Innovation and Entrepreneurship* (London: Pan Books, 1986).

6. J. Masters, President Canadian Hunter Exploration Ltd., from *Exploring De-Organization* (Internal Paper, Nov. 1989), p. 17.

7. S. Wayne, quoted in T. Peters, *Liberation Management*, p. 308.

8. Ibid., p. 682.

10. A WORD OF CAUTION

1. A. Watts, *Tao: The Watercourse Way* (Middlesex, U.K.: Penguin, 1986), p. 107.

11. FACILITATION AND ECONOMIC DEVELOPMENT

1. T. Peters, *Liberation Management*, p. 485.

2. Ibid., p. 485.

3. P. Drucker, *Innovation and Entrepreneurship*, p. 284.

4. E. Schumacher, *A Guide for the Perplexed* (London: Jonathan Cape, 1977), p. 17.

5. Konosuke Matsushita, Executive Advisor of Matsushita Electric Industrial Co. Ltd., from *Off the Cuff* (Internal Paper, 1979).

12. A QUIET REVOLUTION

1. Carl Rogers, *Carl Rogers on Personal Power*, p. 5. Those interested in the possible development of a sociology of health, see A. H. Maslow, C. Rogers, Charles Hampen-Turner and E. Fromm. Founders of the American Association for Humanistic Psychology also include Kurt Goldstein, Rollo May, Lewis Mumford, and J.F.T. Bugental.

2. Ibid., p. 6.

3. Ibid., pp. 7-8.

4. Ibid., pp. 8-9.

5. A.S. Neill, *Summerhill* (London: Penguin, 1970), p. 20.

6. J. Campbell, *The Hero With a Thousand Faces* (Princeton: Princeton University Press, 1979), p. 10.

7. K. Gibran, *The Prophet* (New York: Paladin, 1927).

8. I. Illich, *Deschooling Society* (Middlesex, U.K.; Penguin, 1973), p. 78.

9. D.H. Smith, *Confucius*, p. 76.

13. THE POLITICS OF PERSONAL GROWTH

1. Walt Anderson, *Politics and the New Humanism*, p. 144.

2. J.B. Watson, *Behaviorism* (New York: Norton, 1924), p. 303 fn.

3. B.F. Skinner, *The Behavior of Organisms: An Experimental Analysis* (New York: Appleton Century Croft, 1966), p. 47.

4. Donald M. Baer, "Let's take another look at punishment," *Psychology Today*, Oct. 1971, p. 162.

5. E. Boring, *A History of Experimental Psychology* (New York: Appleton Century Crofts, 1950), p. 645.

6. B.F. Skinner, *Walden Two* (New York: Macmillan, 1948), p. 262.

7. Walt Anderson, *Politics and the New Humanism*, p. 145.

8. A. H. Maslow, quoted in Rollo May and Carl Rogers, *American Politics and Humanistic Psychology* (Dallas: Saybrook Institute Press, 1984), p. 100.

9. F. Perls, R. Hefferline and P. Goodman, *Gestalt Therapy* (New York: Delta, 1965), p. 215.

10. Walt Anderson quoted in Rollo May & Carl Rogers, *American Politics and Humanistic Psychology*, p. 174.

11. I. Illich, *Deschooling Society*, pp. 59-60.

12. Y. Yevtushenko, *Selected Poems* (Penguin, 1962).

14. EPILOGUE: Civic Society, Social Capital, and the Creation of Wealth

1. Dee Hock, *Community Alliance of Interdependent Agriculture*, (Unpublished Paper, 1997).

2. Robert D. Putnam, *Making Democracy Work: Civic Tradition in Modern Italy* (Princeton: Princeton University Press, 1993), p.154.

3. Robert D. Putnam, "The Prosperous Community: Social Capital and Public Life," *The American Prospect* (Spring 1993), p. 36.

4. Ibid., p.36.

5. Ibid., p.37.

6. J.K. Hyde, *Society and Politics in Medieval Italy: Evolution of the Civic Life, 1000 – 1350* (London: MacMillan, 1973), p. 38.

7. Don Herzog, "Some Questions for Republicans", *Political Theory* 14 (1986), p. 473.

151

ABOUT THE AUTHOR

Italian-born Ernesto Sirolli received a Laurea di Dottore in Political Science from Rome University in 1976. For the last 28 years, he has worked in Europe, Africa, Australia, New Zealand, Canada, and the U.S.A. in the field of Local Economic Development.

In 1985, he pioneered in Esperance, a small rural community in Western Australia, a unique social technology based on harnessing the passion, determination, intelligence, and resourcefulness of the local people.

The striking results of "The Esperance Experience" have prompted more than two hundred and fifty communities in four countries to adopt responsive, person-centered approaches to local economic development similar to the Enterprise Facilitation model pioneered in Esperance.

Ernesto Sirolli is the founder of the Sirolli Institute, an international nonprofit organization which teaches community leaders how to establish and mantain Enterprise Facilitation projects in their communities.

* * *

For further information about Enterprise Facilitation, in North America call toll-free 1-877-SIROLLI. See the Web site MACROBUTTON HtmlResAnchor http://www.sirolli.com or email sirolli@visi.com. You will then be directed to offices in other countries.

You can also contact Yvonne Fizer, Sirolli Institute Customer Relations, at Telephone: 1-877-SIROLLI (1-877-747-6554), Fax: (780) 466-0329.

Books to Build a New Society

New Society Publisher's mission is to is to publish books
that contribute in fundamental ways to building an
ecologically sustainable and just society, and to do so with
the least possible impact on the environment
in a manner that models that vision.

We specialize in:

sustainable living

ecological design and planning

environment and justice

nonviolence

resistance and community

the feminist transformation

progressive leadership

accountable economics

conscientious commerce, and

education and parenting resources

For a full catalog, call 1-800-567-6772, or visit our web site at
www.newsociety.com

New Society Publishers